Contents:

5

JavaScript Overview

JavaScript is a programming language that allows you to implement features on web pages or browser to achieve our requirement.

Always, a web page does more than just to display static information or content that we can see on the browser.

Please note, this book only introduces core topics or functions of JavaScript and better to have knowledge about HTML and CSS.

How To Run a JavaScript Program:

Before talking about JavaScript code features or writing a program, we will see how can we run a JavaScript program.

There are below different ways to run a JavaScript code/program:

1. Using web browser console
2. By creating web pages
3. Using node.js
4. Using online JavaScript compiler

Using Console of Web Browser

This way uses mostly for learning purpose. Below are the steps:

   a) Open any browser, here we will continue with Google Chrome
   b) Right click on an empty area and then select Inspect to open the developer tools.

c) In develop tools, select console tab where you can write your JavaScript code and the press 'Enter' key to see the output.

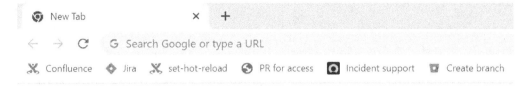

Creating Web Pages

As we know, JavaScript was created to make web pages interactive, so we can run our JavaScript code with by web pages. There is two ways to run the JavaScript code from web pages.

    I) Including your JavaScript within web pages

    II) Linking a JavaScript file in web pages

I) Including your JavaScript within web pages

This is the basic way to write and run JavaScript code/program in a web page inside a script tag. Below are the steps:

    A. Create a file with .html extension using any editor (like: main.html)

B. Add minimum required html and save it

```html
<!doctype html>
<html lang="en">

<head>
    <meta charset="utf-8">
    <title>test program</title>
</head>

<body>
</body>

</html>
```

C. Add <script></script> tag in your file before </head>, it is a better place to add JavaScript code however you can also add your script with in other tags as well.

```html
<!doctype html>
<html lang="en">

<head>
    <meta charset="utf-8">
    <title>test program</title>
    <script>
        document.write("Hello from JavaScript Program.");  //this uses to write something on browser
        console.log("Hello from JavaScript Program."); //this uses to log something on browser console
    </script>
</head>

<body>
</body>

</html>
```

D. Now file looks

```
<> main.html X

<> main.html > ⊘ html > ⊘ head
    1    <!doctype html>
    2    <html lang="en">
    3
    4    <head>
    5        <meta charset="utf-8">
    6        <title>test program</title>
    7        <script>
    8            document.write("Hello from JavaScript Program.");  //this uses to write something on browser
    9            console.log("Hello from JavaScript Program.") //this uses to log something on browser console
   10        </script>
   11    </head>|
   12
   13    <body>
   14    </body>
   15
   16    </html>
```

E. Now open your saved file in any browser it will give you the below result

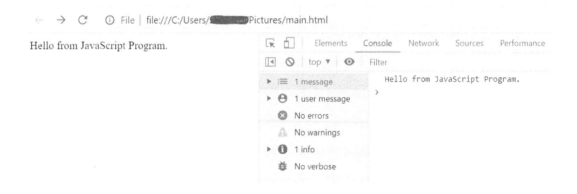

Please note, further we will log anything from our JavaScript program to browser's console using console.log().

II) Linking a JavaScript file in web pages

This is the standard way to use JavaScript code in your web pages.

Below are the steps:

A. Create a file with **.html** extension using any editor (like: **main.html**)

B. Add minimum required html and save it

```
<!doctype html>
<html lang="en">

<head>
    <meta charset="utf-8">
    <title>test program</title>
</head>

<body>
</body>

</html>
```

C. Similar create another new file with **.js** extension and save it (like: **main.js**)

D. Write the below code and save it.

```
document.write("Hello from JavaScript Program.");   //this uses to write
something on browser
console.log("Hello from JavaScript Program."); //this uses to log something on
browser console
```

E. Link your **.js** file inside **.html** file using <script></script> tag and specifying it's scr property.

```
<script src="./main.js"></script>
```

F. Now both file looks like

```
<> main.html X    JS main.js
<> main.html > ⊘ html
  1    <!doctype html>
  2    <html lang="en">
  3
  4    <head>
  5        <meta charset="utf-8">
  6        <title>test program</title>
  7        <script src="./main.js"></script>
  8    </head>
  9
 10    <body>
 11    </body>
 12
 13    </html>
```

```
<> main.html    JS main.js    ✕
JS main.js
    1    document.write("Hello from JavaScript Program.");  //this uses to write something on browser
    2    console.log("Hello from JavaScript Program.") //this uses to log something on browser console
```

G. Open .html file to any browser, it will give you the same result as pervious

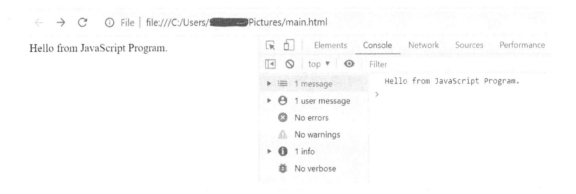

Hello from JavaScript Program.

Using node.js

Node is a JavaScript run-time environment for executing the JavaScript code. Below are the steps:

A. Install Node.JS latest version

B. Install/Open any IDE or editor to create a new file with **.js** extension. (Better to use VS code).

C. Write JavaScript code in file and save it.

```
console.log("Hello from JavaScript Program.");
```

D. Now open your terminal, go to file location and run below command and then press 'Enter' you will see the output on same terminal.

>node filename.js

Using online JavaScript compiler

These days, you can find many online JavaScript compiler sites on internet. You can also use those sites for learning JavaScript. However, this is not a preferred way.

JavaScript Data Types

As we know, Data types is an important feature of any programming language. Without Data Types no language can operate or manage different type of values. Like: Strings, Numbers and more. Hence JavaScript is also having data types to holds the different types of values. But no need to specify data types at the time of variable declaration.

Or we can say "JavaScript is a **dynamic data types language;** means there is no need to specify type of the variable because it is dynamically used by JavaScript internal engine."

So instead of using specific types in front of variables, we can use any below key word.

1. Var
2. Let
3. Const

```
var title = "JavaScript";
console.log(title); //JavaScript

let subTitle = "JavaScript Data Types";
console.log(subTitle); //JavaScript Data Types

const BOOK_NAME = "JavaScript Basics";
console.log(BOOK_NAME); //JavaScript Basics
```

Little confusing when we use which one. No worries we will explain these all-in details in this book after some time.

Now comes on to JavaScript data types:

There are two types of data types in JavaScript.

1. Primitive data type

2. Non-primitive (reference) data type

1. JavaScript Primitive data types

As we already mentioned above, JavaScript data types use by the JavaScript engine to manage the different types of values and perform the operations. There is no need to specify at the time of variable declaration.

Below are the primitive data types in JavaScripts:

1. String
2. Number
3. Boolean
4. Undefined
5. Null

String:

a) String data type represents a sequence of characters.

b) Strings are written with quotes. You can use single or double quotes

```
var title = "JavaScript";
console.log(title); //JavaScript

let name = "John";
console.log(name); //John
```

Number

a) Number data type represent numeric value or digits

b) Quotes are not required

```
var age = 18;
console.log(age); //18
```

Boolean

a) Boolean data type represents Boolean of bit value either **true** or **false**

```
var isTrue = true;
console.log(isTrue); //true

var isEqual = 10 === 10;
console.log(isEqual); //true
```

Undefined

a) Represent undefined value

b) Unassigned variables are initialized by JavaScript automatically with a default value of **undefined**.

```
var test;
console.log(test); //undefined
```

Null

a) Represent Null value

b) **null** is an object. It can be assigned to a variable as a representation of no value.

```
var test = null;
console.log(test); //null
```

Please note, we can check data type of a variable using **typeof** operator of JavaScript.

```
let name = "John";
let age = 23;
let isMale = true;
let address = null;
let city;

console.log(typeof name); //string
console.log(typeof age); //number
console.log(typeof isMale); //boolean
console.log(typeof address); //object
console.log(typeof city); //undefined
```

2. JavaScript Non-Primitive data types

Below are the non-primitive data types in JavaScript:

JavaScript Object:

a) Object represent an instance or a group of properties and methods.

b) Object can contain many values

```
const car = { type: "fiat", model: 500, color: "white" }
console.log(car); //{ type: 'fiat', model: 500, color: 'white' }
//read property value
console.log(car.type); //fiat
```

Creating object in JavaScript:

a) Using object literal

```
let car = { type: "fiat", model: 500, color: "white" }
console.log(typeof car);
//read property value
console.log(car.type, car.model, car.color);
//output:
//object
//fiat 500 white
```

b) Using JavaScript Object constructor

```
let car = new Object({ type: "fiat", model: 500, color: "white" });
car.price = '$10000';
console.log(typeof car);
//read property value
console.log(car.type, car.model, car.color, car.price);
//output:
//object
//fiat 500 white $10000
```

c) Using function/object constructor

```
function car(type, model, color, price) {
    this.type = type;
    this.model = model;
    this.color = color;
    this.price = getPrice;
    function getPrice() {
        return '$' + price;
    }
}
let carObj = new car('fiat', 500, 'white', 10000)
//read property value
console.log(carObj.type, carObj.model, carObj.color, carObj.price());
  //output: fiat 500 white $10000
```

Please note, the 'this' keyword refers to the current object. We will study this keyword in detail later.

Below are some important methods of JavaScript Object:

Object.create():

This method is used to create a new object from an existing object. Which is used same as the prototype of the newly created object.

Syntax:

Object.create(prototype)

Object.create(prototype, propertiesObject)

Example 1:

```
const car = {
    getInfo: function () {
        return this.type + ' ' + this.model;
    }
}
const obj = Object.create(car);
obj.type = "fiat";
obj.model = 500;
console.log(obj.getInfo())
  // output: fiat 500
```

Example 2:

```
const car = {
    getInfo: function () {
        return this.type + ' ' + this.model;
    }
}
const obj = Object.create(car, { type: { value: "fiat" } });
obj.model = 500;
console.log(obj.getInfo())
  // output: fiat 500
```

Please note we can only define a property in a property object using property descriptors. It may optionally contain the following keys:

configurable : Default value is false. Set it to true if the property may be deleted from object in future or the type may change.

Example:

```
const car = {}
const obj = Object.create(car, {
  type : { value : "fiat",configurable : true, enumerable : true},
  model : { value : 500, enumerable : true}
});
console.log(obj)
delete obj.model;
delete obj.type;
console.log(obj)
// output:
//{ type: 'fiat', model: 500 }
//{ model: 500 }
```

Enumerable: Default value is false. Set it to true then this property displays during emuration of the corresponding object properties.

Example:

```
const car = {}
const obj = Object.create(car, {
  type : { value : "fiat"},
  model : { value : 500, enumerable : true}
});
console.log(obj)
// output:
//{ model: 500 }
```

value: Default value is undefined. However, we can assign any value to property.

writable: Default value is false. Set it to true if property value may change in future using assignment operator.

Example:

```javascript
const car = {}
const obj = Object.create(car, {
  type : { value : "fiat", enumerable : true, writable : true},
  model : { value : 500, enumerable : true}
});
obj.type = "sudaan"; //can change
obj.model = 1000; //cannot change
console.log(obj)
// output:
//{ type: 'sudaan', model: 500 }
```

get: this is a getter function which return the value for the property.

Example:

```javascript
const car = {}
let value = 20;
const obj = Object.create(car, {
    type: { value: "fiat", enumerable: true, writable: true },
    model: {
        enumerable: true, get() {
            return value;
        }
    }
});
obj.type = "sudaan"; //can change
obj.model = 500; //cannot change
console.log(obj.model)
// output: 20
```

set: this is a setter function which uses to set the value of property.

Example:

```
const car = {}
let value = 20;
const obj = Object.create(car, {
    type: { value: "fiat", enumerable: true, writable: true },
    model: {
        enumerable: true, get() {
            return value;
        },
        set(newValue) {
            value = newValue;
        }
    }
});
obj.type = "sudaan"; //can change
obj.model = 500; //can change
console.log(obj.model)
// output: 500
```

Please note, in a property descriptor, we cannot both specify accessors(get/set) and a value or writable attribute at same time.

Object.assign():

This method is used to copy all enumerable own properties from one or more source objects to a target object and returns the modified target object.

If target object and sources object have the same properties then target object properties are overwritten with sources objects properties and last source properties have more precedence than any other.

Syntax:

Object.assign(target, source1[, source2,…,sourceN])

Example:

```
const target = { };
const source1 = { a: 5, b: 6 };
const source2 = { b: 7, c: 8 };
const returnedTarget = Object.assign(target, source1, source2);
console.log(target);
console.log(returnedTarget === target);
// output:
//{ a: 5, b: 7, c: 8 }
//true
```

Object.defineProperty():

This method is used to define a new property or overwrite an existing property on an object using property descriptor and return the modified object.

Syntax:

Object.defineProperty(object, property, propertyDescriptor)

Example:

```
const car = {type:"sudaan"}
let obj = Object.defineProperty(car,"type", {
  value : "fiat",
  enumerable : true,
  writable : false});
obj = Object.defineProperty(car, "model", {
  value : 500,
  enumerable : true,
  writable : false});
console.log(car)
console.log(car === obj)
// output:
//{ type: 'fiat', model: 500 }
//true
```

Object.defineProperties():

This method is used to define multiple new property or overwrite existing properties on an object using property descriptors and return the modified object.

Syntax:

Object.defineProperties(object, propertyObject)

Example:

```
const car = {type:"sudaan"}
let obj = Object.defineProperties(car, {
  type : {value : "fiat",
  enumerable : true,
  writable : false},
  model : {
  value : 500,
  enumerable : true,
  writable : false}
  });
console.log(car)
console.log(car === obj)
// output:
//{ type: 'fiat', model: 500 }
//true
```

Object.freeze():

This method is used to prevent existing properties of an object from being removed, modified and new properties from being added.

Syntax:

Object.freeze(object)

Example:

```
const car = {type:"sudaan", model : 500}
delete car.type; //can delete
car.model = 600; //can modified
car.price = 500; //can add
console.log(car);
const obj = Object.freeze(car);
delete car.model; //cannot delete
car.type = "sudaan"; //cannot add
car.price = 700; //cannot modified
console.log(car);
console.log(car === obj);
// output:
//{ model: 600, price: 500 }
//{ model: 600, price: 500 }
//true
```

Object.entries():

It creates an iterator object as key/value pair.

Syntax:

Object.entries(object)

Example:

```
const car = {type:"sudaan", model : 500}
const entries = Object.entries(car);
for(let entry of entries)
console.log(entry)
// output:
//[ 'type', 'sudaan' ]
//[ 'model', 500 ]
```

Object.getOwnPropertyDescriptor():
This method returns an object of a property descriptor for the own property of the given object.

Syntax:
Object.getOwnPropertyDescriptor(object, property_name);

Example:

```js
const car = { type: "sudaan", model: 500 }
const typeDescriptor = Object.getOwnPropertyDescriptor(car, "type");
console.log(typeDescriptor)
// output:
/*{
  value: 'sudaan',
  writable: true,
  enumerable: true,
  configurable: true
}*/
```

Object.getOwnPropertyDescriptors():

This method returns an object contains all own property descriptors of a specified object.

Syntax:

Object.getOwnPropertyDescriptors(object)

Example:

```js
const car = { type: "sudaan", model: 500 }
const propDescriptors = Object.getOwnPropertyDescriptors(car);
console.log(propDescriptors)
// output:
/*{
  type: {
    value: 'sudaan',
    writable: true,
    enumerable: true,
    configurable: true
  },
  model: {
  value: 500,
  writable: true,
  enumerable: true,
  configurable: true
  }
}*/
```

Object.getOwnPropertyNames():

This method returns all properties of an object in form of array.

Syntax:

Object.getOwnPropertyNames(object)

Example:

```
const car = {type:"sudaan", model : 500}
const propNames = Object.getOwnPropertyNames(car);
console.log(propNames)
// output:
//[ 'type', 'model' ]
```

Object.getPrototypeOf():

This method is used to get prototype of a given object.

Syntax:

Object.getPrototypeOf(object)

Example:

```
const car = {type:"sudaan", model : 500}
const obj = Object.create(car);
const _prototype = Object.getPrototypeOf(obj);
console.log(_prototype)
// output:
//{ type: 'sudaan', model: 500 }
```

Object.keys():

This method is used to get object's own property names.

Syntax:

Object.keys(object)

Example:

```
const car = {type:"sudaan", model : 500}
const propNames = Object.keys(car);
console.log(propNames)
// output:
//[ 'type', 'model' ]
```

Object.is():

This method compares whether two values are the same value.

Syntax:

Object.is(value1,value2)

Example:

```
console.log(Object.is(1,1))
console.log(Object.is(1,'1'))
console.log(Object.is(null, null));
console.log(Object.is(undefined, undefined));
console.log(Object.is({type:"fiat"},{type:"fiat"}))
// output:
//true
//false
//true
//true
//false
```

Object.isExtensible():

This method returns true if an object is extensible else returns false.

Syntax:

Object.isExtensible(object)

Example:

```
const car = {type:"sudaan", model : 500}
console.log(Object.isExtensible(car));
Object.seal(car);
console.log(Object.isExtensible(car));
// output:
//true
//false
```

Object.isFrozen():

This method returns true if an object was frozen else return false.

Syntax:

Object.freeze(object)

Example:

```
const car = {type:"sudaan", model : 500}
const obj = Object.freeze(car);
console.log(Object.isFrozen(car));
console.log(Object.isFrozen(obj));
// output:
//true
//true
```

Object.isSealed():

This method returns true if an object is sealed else return false.

Syntax:

Object.isSealed(object)

Example:

```
const car = {type:"sudaan", model : 500}
console.log(Object.isSealed(car));
Object.seal(car);
console.log(Object.isSealed(car));
// output:
//false
//true
```

Object.preventExtensions():

This method is used to prevent new properties from being added but existing properties can be deleted and modified.

Syntax:

Object.preventExtensions(object)

Example:

```
const car = {type:"sudaan", model : 500}
car.price = 600; //can add
car.model = 700; //can modify
delete car.type; //can delete
console.log(car);
Object.preventExtensions(car);
car.type = "fiat"; //cannot add
car.model = 800; //can modify
delete car.price; //can delete
console.log(car);
// output:
//{ model: 700, price: 600 }
//{ model: 800 }
```

Object.seal():

This method is used to prevent new properties from being added and existing properties from being removed.

Syntax:
Object.seal(object)

Example:

```javascript
const car = {type:"sudaan", model : 500}
car.price = 500; //can add
delete car.model; //can delete
console.log(car);
Object.seal(car);
car.price = 600; //can modify
car.model = 200; //cannot add
delete car.price; //cannot delete
console.log(car);
// output:
//{ type: 'sudaan', price: 500 }
//{ type: 'sudaan', price: 600 }
```

Object.setPrototypeOf():

This method sets the prototype of a target object from source object.

Syntax:

Object.setPrototypeOf(targetObject, sourceObject);

Example:

```javascript
const subCar = {};
const car = { type: "fiat" };
console.log(subCar.type);
Object.setPrototypeOf(subCar, car);
console.log(subCar.type);
//output:
//undefined
//fiat
```

Object.values():

This method is used to get an array of all properties value.

Syntax:

Object.values(object)

Example:

```
const car = { type: "fiat", model: 500 };
const values = Object.values(car);
console.log(values);
//output: [ 'fiat', 500 ]
```

JavaScript Array object:

    a)   Array represents a collection of similar type values

    b)   We can set or get a value from array using index

```
const names = ["john", "jim", "tim"];
console.log(names); //["john", "jim", "tim"]

//get value
console.log(names[2]); //tim

//set value
names[2] = "kane";
console.log(names[2]); //kane
```

Create an array using new keyword:

```
const names = new Array("john", "jim", "tim");
console.log(names); //["john", "jim", "tim"]

//get value
console.log(names[2]); //tim

//set value
names[2] = "kane";
console.log(names[2]); //kane
```

Below are important methods of Array:

Please note, some of the methods takes **startIndex**, **endIndex** and **endPosition** as parameters.

Index always start from 0 and position starts from 1. **which means index = 0 and position = 1 point the first/same element of an array.**

concat():

It merges two or more arrays and return a new merged array.

Syntax:

array.concat(arr_1,arr_2,...,arr_n)

Example:

```
let arr1 = [1, 2, 3];
let arr2 = [4, 5, 6];
console.log(arr1.concat(arr2))
//output : [ 1, 2, 3, 4, 5, 6 ]
```

copywithin():

It copies sub part of given array with its own elements and returns the modified array.

Syntax:

array.copyWithin(targetIndex, startIndex, endPosition)

Example:

```
var arr = ["JavaScript", "CSS", "JQuery", "Bootstrap"];
console.log(arr.copyWithin(0, 2, 3))
//output : [ 'JQuery', 'CSS', 'JQuery', 'Bootstrap' ]
```

entries():

It creates an iterator object as key/value pair.

Syntax:

array.entries()

Example:

```
var arr = ["JavaScript", "CSS", "JQuery", "Bootstrap"];
let entries = arr.entries();
for (let entry of entries)
    console.log(entry)
/*
Output :
[ 0, 'JavaScript' ]
[ 1, 'CSS' ]
[ 2, 'JQuery' ]
[ 3, 'Bootstrap' ] */
```

every():

It returns true if all the elements of an array are satisfying the provided function conditions else return false.

Example:

```
var marks = [30, 20, 50];
function isGreaterThan(ele, value) {
    return ele > value
}
console.log(marks.every(ele => isGreaterThan(ele, 20)))
//output: false
```

flat():

It creates a new flat array based on the sub-array elements recursively till the specified depth.

Syntax:

array.flat(depth)

Example:

```
var arr = [[30, 20, [40]], [50]];
console.log(arr.flat(1))
console.log(arr.flat(2))
/*
output:
[ 30, 20, [ 40 ], 50 ]
[ 30, 20, 40, 50 ] */
```

flatMap():

It maps all array elements via mapping function, then returns a new flat array.

Example:

```
var arr1 = [10, 20];
var arr2 = [30, 40];
console.log(arr1.flatMap((arr1, index) => [arr1, arr2[index]]))
//output: [ 10, 30, 20, 40 ]
```

fill():

It fills elements on specified indexes into an array with static values.

Syntax:

Array.fill(element, [startIndex, endPosition])

Example:

```
var arr1 = [10, 20, 30, 40];
console.log(arr1.fill(5, 1, 3))
//output: [ 10, 5, 5, 40 ]
```

from():

It creates a new array based on another array elements.

Syntax:

Array.from(array)

34

Example:

```
var arr1 = [10, 20, 30, 40];
var newArr = Array.from(arr1);
var newArr1 = Array.from("Thank you!");
console.log(newArr)
console.log(newArr1)
/*
output:
[ 10, 20, 30, 40 ]
['T', 'h', 'a', 'n', 'k', ' ', 'y', 'o', 'u', '!'] */
```

filter():

It returns the new array containing the elements that satisfy the provided function conditions.

Example:

```
var arr1 = [10, 20, 30, 40];
var newArr = arr1.filter((ele, index, arr1) => ele > 20);
console.log(newArr)
// output: [ 30, 40 ]
```

find():

It returns the first element in the given array that satisfies the provided function condition.

Example:

```
var arr1 = [10, 50, 30, 40];
var value = arr1.find((ele, index, arr1) => ele > 20);
console.log(value)
// output: 50
```

findIndex():

It returns the index of the first element in the given array that satisfies the provided function condition.

Example:

```
let arr1 = [0, 2, 30, 40];
let index = arr1.findIndex((ele, index, arr) => ele === 30);
console.log(index)
// output: 2
```

forEach():

It invokes the provided function once for each element of the given array.

Example:

```
let arr1 = [0, 2, 30, 40];
arr1.forEach((ele, index, arr1) => {
    console.log(index, '-', ele);
})
/*
output:
0 - 0
1 - 2
2 - 30
3 - 40 */
```

includes():

It returns true if the given array contains the specified element else return false.

Syntax:

array.includes(ele)

Example:

```
let arr1=[0, 2, 30, 40];
console.log(arr1.includes(30));
console.log(arr1.includes(70));
// output:
//true
//false
```

indexOf():

It returns the index of the first match else return –1.

Syntax:

Array.indexOf(element)

Example:

```
let arr1=[0, 2, 30, 40];
console.log(arr1.indexOf(30));
console.log(arr1.indexOf(70));
// output:
//2
//-1
```

isArray():

It tests if the passed value is an array.

Syntax:

Array.isArray(obj)

Example:

```
let arr1 = [0, 2, 30, 40];
console.log(Array.isArray(arr1));
// output: true
```

join():

It joins the elements of an array as a string.

Syntax:

array.join(delemeter)

Example:

```
let arr1 = [0, 2, 30, 40];
console.log(arr1.join('|'));
// output: 0|2|30|40
```

keys():

It creates an iterator object that contains only the keys of the array, then loops through these keys.

Syntax:

array.keys()

Example:

```
let arr1=[0, 2, 30, 40];
let keys = arr1.keys();
for(let key of keys)
console.log(key);
// output:
// 0
// 1
// 2
// 3
```

lastIndexOf():

It returns the index of the last match element else return –1.

Syntax:

array.lastIndexOf(element)

Example:

```
let arr1 = [0, 2, 30, 40, 30, 50, 30];
console.log(arr1.lastIndexOf(30));
// output: 6
```

map():

It calls the provided function for every array element and returns the newly created array.

Example:

```
let arr1 = [1, 2, 3];
let newArray = arr1.map((ele, index, arr1) => ele * 2)
console.log(newArray);
// output: [ 2, 4, 6 ]
```

of():

It creates a new array from the passed arguments, holding any type of argument.

Example:

```
let arr1 = Array.of(1, 2, 3, 4);
console.log(arr1);
// output: [ 1, 2, 3, 4 ]
```

pop():

It removes and returns the last element of an array.

Syntax:

array.pop()

Example:

```
let arr1 = [1, 2, 3, 4]
console.log(arr1.pop());
// output: 4
```

push():

It adds one or more elements to the end of an array.

Syntax:

array.push(element)

Example:

```
let arr1 = [1, 2, 3, 4]
arr1.push(6);
console.log(arr1);
// output: [ 1, 2, 3, 4, 6 ]
```

reverse():

It reverses the elements of given array.

Syntax:

array.reverse()

Example:

```
let arr1 = [1, 2, 4, 3]
console.log(arr1.reverse());
// output: [ 3, 4, 2, 1 ]
```

reduce(function, initial):

It executes a provided function for each value from left to right and returns a single value based on function implementation.

Example:

```
let arr = [1, 2, 3, 4];
let sum = arr.reduce((acc, ele, index, arr) => acc + ele, 5);
console.log(sum);
// Output: 15
```

reduceRight():

It is similar to reduce. It executes a provided function for each value from right to left and returns a single value.

Example:

```
let arr = [1, 2, 3, 4];
let sum = arr.reduceRight((acc, ele, index, arr)=>{
    console.log(index);
    return acc+ele;
    },5);
console.log(sum);
// Output:
// 3
// 2
// 1
// 0
// 15
```

some():

It returns true if the any element of given array satisfies the provided function condition else return false.

Example:

```
let arr = [10, 20, 30, 40];
let isExist = arr.some((ele, index, arr) => ele > 30)
let isExist1 = arr.some((ele, index, arr) => ele > 40)
console.log(isExist, isExist1);
// Output: true false
```

shift():

It removes and returns the first element of an array.

Syntax:

array.shift()

Example:

```
let arr = [10, 20, 30, 40];
let ele = arr.shift();
console.log(ele);
console.log(arr);
// Output:
//10
//[ 20, 30, 40 ]
```

slice():

It returns a new array containing the specified range of the given array.

Syntax:

array.slice(startIndex, endPosition)

Example:

```
let arr = [10, 20, 30, 40];
let newArr = arr.slice(2, 3);
console.log(newArr);
console.log(arr);
// Output:
//[ 30 ]
//[ 10, 20, 30, 40 ]
```

sort():

It returns the element of the given array in a sorted order.

Syntax:

array.sort()

Example:

```
let arr = [10, 40, 30, 20];
arr.sort();
console.log(arr);
// Output:
//[ 10, 20, 30, 40 ]
```

splice():

It add/remove elements to/from the given array based on the specified indexes.

Syntax:

array.splice(startIndex, endIndex)

Example:

```
let arr = [1, 2, 3, 4, 5];
let newArr = arr.splice(2, 4);
console.log(arr);
console.log(newArr);
// Output:
//[ 1, 2 ]
//[ 3, 4, 5 ]
```

toLocaleString():

It returns a string containing all the elements of a specified array and formatted element based on the locale.

Syntax:

array.toLocaleString()

Example:

```
let arr = [1000, 2000, 3000, 4000, 5000];
let str = arr.toLocaleString();
console.log(str);
// Output:
//1,000,2,000,3,000,4,000,5,000
```

toString():

It converts the elements of a specified array into string form, without affecting the original array.

Syntax:

array. toString()

Example:

```
let arr = [1000, 2000, 3000, 4000, 5000];
let str = arr.toString();
console.log(str);
// Output:
//1000,2000,3000,4000,5000
```

unshift():

It adds one or more elements in the beginning of the given array and returns the length.

Syntax:

Array.unshift(ele1, ele2,...,eleN)

Example:

```
let arr = [1000, 2000];
let length = arr.unshift(100, 200);
console.log(arr);
console.log(length);
// Output:
//[ 100, 200, 1000, 2000 ]
//4
```

values():

It creates a new iterator object carrying values for each index in the array.

Example:

```
let arr = [1000, 2000];
let values = arr.values();
for (let value of values)
    console.log(value);
// Output:
// 1000
// 2000
```

Please note, some methods of array are not easily understandable from the above table (like: filter, reduce, sort, map and more). No worries we will discuss these important functions in detail later.

JavaScript String object:

   a) String data type represents a sequence of characters.

   b) Strings are written with quotes. You can use single or double quotes.

   c) We can initialize a string using String constructor as below.

```
let str = new String("this is an apple");
console.log(str);
//output:
//[String: 'this is an apple']
```

Below are some important methods of JavaScript String.

concat():

It returns the new string after concatenates the two or more strings.

Syntax:

str.concat(str1, str2,…,strN)

Example:

```
let str1 = "this is";
let str2 = " an";
let str3 = " apple";
let finalStr = str1.concat(str2, str3);
console.log(finalStr);
//output: this is an apple
```

indexOf():

It returns the first occurrence index of a specified char present in the given string.

Syntax:

str.indexOf(character)

Example:

```
let str = "this is an apple";
let indexOfA = str.indexOf('a');
console.log("Index of a is", indexOfA);
//output: Index of a is  8
```

lastIndexOf():

It returns the last occurrence index of a specified char present in the given string.

Syntax:

str.l.lastIndexOf(stIndexOf(character))

Example:

```
let str = "this is an apple";
let lastIndexOfA = str.lastIndexOf('a');
console.log("Last index of a is", lastIndexOfA);
//output: Last index of a is 11
```

charAt():

It returns the char value present at the given index.

Syntax:

str.charAt(index)

Example:

```
let str = "this is an apple";
let char = str.charAt(8);
console.log("char at index 8 =", char);
//output: char at index 8 = a
```

charCodeAt():

It returns the Unicode value of a character present at the given index.

Syntax:

str. CharCodeAt(index)

Example:

```
let str = "this is an apple";
let charCode = str.charCodeAt(8);
console.log("char code at index 8 =", charCode);
//output: char code at index 8 = 97
```

replace():

It returns new string after replacing a given actual string with the specified replacement string.

Syntax:

str.replace(actualSubString|regex, newReplacementString)

Please note:

By default, this method searches the sub string in a given string using **case-sensitive** behavior and replaces the first occurence. However, when we use search method with **regex parameter** then we can change this behavior using regex flag. it supports all the regex flag.

Example:

```
let str = "this is an apple";
let newString = str.replace("apple","orange");
let newString1 = str.replace(/Is/gi,"orange");
console.log("Actual string =",str);
console.log("New string after replacement =",newString);
console.log("New string after regex replacement =",newString1);
//output:
//New string after replacement = this is an orange
//New string after regex replacement = thorange orange an apple
```

substr():

It is used to get a sub part/string from given string based on the specified index and length.

Syntax:

str.substr(startIndex, length)

Example:

```
let str = "this is an apple";
let subStr = str.substr(11, 5);
console.log("Actual string =",str);
console.log("Sub string =",subStr);
//output:
//Actual string = this is an apple
//Sub string = apple
```

substring():

It is used to get a sub part/string from the given string based on the startIndex and endPosition.

Syntax:

str.subString(startIndex/endPosition, startIndex/endPosition)

Please note:

Above method takes smaller value as startIndex and other as endPosition either it may be passed in any sequence.

Example:

```
let str = "this_is_an_apple";
let subStr = str.substring(5,0);
let subStr1 = str.substring(5,11);
console.log(subStr);
console.log(subStr1);
//output:
//this_
//is_an_
```

slice():

It is used to get a sub part/string from the given string based on the startIndex and endPosition. The parameters can take either positive or negative valuel.

Syntax:

str.slice(startIndex, endPosition)

Please note:

1. We can pass any parameter value as negative which JavaScript interpreter internally converted as below:

```
str.slice(-5, -3)
```

Converted to:

```
str.slice(str.length-5, str.length-3)
```

Let's assume string length is 16 then it looks like:

```
str.slice(11, 13)
```

Start index must be less than the endPosition otherwise method will return a blank string.

Example:

```
let str = "this_is_an_apple";
let subStr = str.slice(5, 7);
let subStr1 = str.slice(-5, 13);
let subStr2 = str.slice(5,-3);
let subStr3 = str.slice(-5, -3);
console.log("str = ", str);
console.log("subStr = ", subStr);
console.log("subStr1 = ", subStr1);
console.log("subStr2 = ", subStr2);
console.log("subStr3 = ", subStr3);
//output:
//str =   this_is_an_apple
//subStr =   is
//subStr1 =   ap
//subStr2 =   is_an_ap
//subStr3 =   ap
```

search():

It searches a specified sub string or regular expression in a given string and returns its position if a match occurs. If a match is not found then return -1.

Syntax:

str.search(string | regex)

Please note:

By default, this method searches the sub string in a given string using **case-sensitive** behavior. However, when we use search method with **regex parameter** then we can change this behavior using regex flag. it supports all the regex flag.

Example:

```
let str = "this_is_an_apple";
let searchIndexAn = str.search('an');
let searchIndexIs = str.search(/Is/i);
console.log(searchIndexAn);
console.log(searchIndexIs);
//output:
//8
//2
```

match():

It searches a specified sub string or regular expression in a given string and returns regular expression if a match occurs. If a match is not found then null.

Syntax:

str.search(string|regex)

Please note:

By default, this method searches the sub string in a given string using **case-sensitive** behavior. However, when we use search method with **regex parameter** then we can change this behavior using regex flag. it supports all the regex flag.

Example:

```
let str = "this_is_an_apple";
let searchIndexAn = str.match('an');
let searchIndexIs = str.match(/Is/gi);
console.log(searchIndexAn);
console.log(searchIndexIs);
//output:
//[ 'an', index: 8, input: 'this_is_an_apple', groups: undefined ]
//[ 'is', 'is' ]
```

toLowerCase():

It converts the string into lowercase.

Syntax:

str.toLowerCase()

Example:

```
let str = "THIS IS AN APPLE";
let newString = str.toLowerCase();
console.log(newString);
//output:
//this is an apple
```

toUpperCase():

It converts the string into uppercase.

Syntax:

str.toUpperCase()

Example:

```
let str = "this is an apple";
let newString = str.toUpperCase();
console.log(newString);
//output:
//THIS IS AN APPLE
```

split():

It splits a given string into sub string array, then returns that newly created array.

Syntax:

str.split(string|regex)

Please note:

By default, this method searches the sub string in a given string using **case-sensitive** behavior. However, when we use search method with **regex parameter** then we can change this behavior using regex flag. it supports all the regex flag.

Example:

```
let str = "this is an apple";
let strArray = str.split(' ');
let strArray1 = str.split(/Is/i);
console.log(strArray);
console.log(strArray1);
//output:
//[ 'this', 'is', 'an', 'apple' ]
//[ 'th', ' ', ' an apple' ]
```

trim():

It removes the white space from the left and right side of the given string.

Syntax:

Str.trim()

Example:

```
let str = "    this is an apple    ";
let newStr = str.trim();
console.log("str =", str ,"$");
console.log("newStr =", newStr ,"$");
//output:
//str =    this is an apple    $
//newStr = this is an apple $
```

valueOf():

It returns the literal value of string object.

Syntax:

strObj.valueOf()

Example:

```
let str = new String("this is an apple");
let strValue = str.valueOf();
console.log("str =", str);
console.log("strValue =", strValue);
//output:
//str = [String: 'this is an apple']
//strValue = this is an apple
```

toString():

It returns a string representing the particular object.

Syntax:

strObj.toString()

Example:

```
let str = new String("this is an apple");
let strVal1 = str.toString();
console.log(typeof str);
console.log(typeof strVal1);
//output:
//object
//string
```

JavaScript Number object

a)   Number data type represent numeric value or digits

b)   Quotes are not required

c)   We can initialize a number using Number constructor as well.

```
let number = new Number(5.5); //initialize using constructor
console.log(number);
let number1 = 5.5;   //number literals
console.log(number1);
//output:
//[Number: 5.5]
//5.5
```

Below are some important JavaScript number constants.

Constants	Description	Example
MAX_VALUE	It returns the largest maximum value.	`console.log(Number.MAX_VALUE)` `//output : 1.7976931348623157e+308`
MIN_VALUE	It returns the largest minimum value.	`console.log(Number.MIN_VALUE)` `//output : 5e-324`
POSITIVE_INFINITY	It returns positive infinity	`console.log(Number.POSITIVE_INFINITY)` `//output : Infinity`
NEGATIVE_INFINITY	It returns negative infinity	`console.log(Number.NEGATIVE_INFINITY)` `//output : -Infinity`
NaN	It represents "Not a Number" value.	`console.log(Number.NaN)` `//output : NaN`

Below are some important methods of JavaScript Number:

valueOf():

It returns the literal value of Number object.

Syntax:

number.valueOf()

Example:

```
let int_value1 = new Number(5);
let float_value1 = new Number(5.5);
console.log(int_value1.valueOf())
console.log(float_value1.valueOf())
//output :
//5
//5.5
```

isFinite():

It returns true whether the given value is a finite number else return false.

Syntax:

number.isFinite(value)

Example:

```
let value = 5;
let infiniteValue = Number.POSITIVE_INFINITY;
let value1 = new Number(5);
let infiniteValue1 = new Number(Number.POSITIVE_INFINITY);
console.log(Number.isFinite(value))
console.log(Number.isFinite(infiniteValue))
console.log(Number.isFinite(value1.valueOf()))
console.log(Number.isFinite(infiniteValue1.valueOf()))
//output :
//true
//false
//true
//false
```

isInteger():

It returns true whether the given value is an integer number else return false.

Syntax:

number.isInteger(value)

Example:

```
let int_value = 5;
let float_value = 5.5;
let int_value1 = new Number(5);
let float_value1 = new Number(5.5);
console.log(Number.isInteger(int_value))
console.log(Number.isInteger(float_value))
console.log(Number.isInteger(int_value1.valueOf()))
console.log(Number.isInteger(float_value1.valueOf()))
//output :
//true
//false
//true
//false
```

parseFloat():

It converts the given string into a floating-point number else return NaN.

Syntax:

Number.parseFloat(str1)

Example:

```
let value = "5.5";
let str = "stri50ng78";
let str1 = "75string";
let str2 = "75.25string";
console.log(Number.parseFloat(value))
console.log(Number.parseFloat(str))
console.log(Number.parseFloat(str1))
console.log(Number.parseFloat(str2))
//output :
//5.5
//NaN
//75
//75.25
```

parseInt():

It converts the given string into a floating-point number else return NaN.

Syntax:

Number.parseInt(str1)

Example:

```
let value = "5.5";
let str = "stri50ng78";
let str1 = "75string";
let str2 = "75.25string";
console.log(Number.parseInt(value))
console.log(Number.parseInt(str))
console.log(Number.parseInt(str1))
console.log(Number.parseInt(str2))
//output :
//5
//NaN
//75
//75
```

toExponential():

It returns exponential notation in form of string of the given number.

Syntax:

number.toExponential()

Example:

```
let value = 5.5;
console.log(value.toExponential())
console.log(typeof value.toExponential())
//output :
//5.5e+0
//string
```

toFixed():

It returns the string representation of a number with exact number of decimal digits.

Syntax:

number. toFixed(count)

Example:

```
let value = 5.5555;
console.log(value.toFixed(2))
console.log(typeof value.toFixed(2))
//output :
//5.56
//string
```

toString():

It returns the string representation of a given number

Syntax:

number.toString([base])

Please note:

Default value of base is 10. However, we can also specify base value. Like: For octal, it should be 8, for binary it should be 2 and so on.

Example:

```
let value = 34;
console.log(value.toString())
console.log(value.toString(8))
console.log(typeof value.toString())
//output :
//34
//42
//string
```

JavaScript Math object:

The **JavaScript math** object allows us to perform mathematical operations on numbers.   it provides several constants and methods. JavaScript Math object doesn't have constructors.

Example:

let's suppose we want to get absolute value of a given number then we can get this using abs() method of Math object.

```
let number = new Number(-5.5);
let number1 = -20;
console.log(Math.abs(number));
console.log(Math.abs(number1));
//output:
//5.5
//20
```

Below are some important methods of Math object:

abs():

It returns the absolute value of the given value if value is convertible to number else returns NaN.

Syntax:

Math.abs(value)

Example:

```
let number = new Number(-5.5);
let number1 = "-20";
let string = "-20Mangos";
console.log(Math.abs(number));
console.log(Math.abs(number1));
console.log(Math.abs(string));
//output:
//5.5
//20
//NaN
```

ceil():

It returns a closest integer value, greater than or equal to the given value/number if value is convertible to number else returns NaN.

Syntax:

Math. **ceil** (value)

Example:

```
let number = new Number(-5.6);
let number1 = "20.4";
let string = "-20Mangos";
console.log(Math.ceil(number));
console.log(Math.ceil(number1));
console.log(Math.ceil(string));
//output:
//-5
//21
//NaN
```

floor():

It returns a closest integer value, less than or equal to the given value/number if value is convertible to number else returns NaN.

Syntax:

Math.**floor**(value)

Example:

```
let number = new Number(-5.6);
let number1 = "20.4";
let string = "-20Mangos";
console.log(Math.floor(number));
console.log(Math.floor(number1));
console.log(Math.floor(string));
//output:
//-6
//20
//NaN
```

exp():

It returns the exponential form of the given value if value is convertible to number else returns NaN.

Syntax:

Math.**exp**(value)

Example:

```
let number = 20.4;
let number1 = "20.4";
let string = "-20Mangos";
console.log(Math.exp(number));
console.log(Math.exp(number1));
console.log(Math.exp(string));
//output:
//723781420.9482772
//723781420.9482772
//NaN
```

max():

It returns maximum value of the given values if all values are convertible to numbers else returns NaN.

Syntax:

Math.max(value1,value2,...,valueN)

Example:

```
let number = 2.4;
let number1 = "20.4";
let string = "-20Mangos";
console.log(Math.max(number, number1));
console.log(Math.max(number, number1, string));
//output:
//20.4
//723781420.9482772
```

min():

It returns minimum value of the given values if all values are convertible to numbers else returns NaN.

Syntax:

Math.min(value1,value2,…,valueN)

Example:

```
let number = 2.4;
let number1 = "20.4";
let string = "-20Mangos";
console.log(Math.min(number, number1));
console.log(Math.min(number, number1, string));
//output:
//2.4
//NaN
```

pow():

It returns value of base to the power of exponent if the both parameters (base and **exponent**) are convertible to numbers else return NaN.

Syntax:

Math.pow(base, exponent)

Example:

```
let number = 2;
let number1 = "20";
let string = "-20Mangos";
console.log(Math.pow(number, 2));
console.log(Math.pow(number1, "2"));
console.log(Math.pow(string, 2));
//output:
//4
//400
//NaN
```

round():

It returns a closest integer value to the given value/number if value is convertible to number else returns NaN.

Syntax:

Math.round(value)

Example:

```
let number = 2.4;
let number1 = "20.6";
let string = "-20Mangos";
console.log(Math.round(number));
console.log(Math.round(number1));
console.log(Math.round(string));
//output:
//2
//21
//NaN
```

random():

It returns a random number between range 0 (inclusive) to 1 (exclusive).

Syntax:

Math.random()

Example:

```
console.log(Math.random());
//output:
//any value b/w 0 (inclusive) to 1 (exclusive)
```

sqrt():

It returns the square root of the given value if it is positive and convertible to a number else return NaN.

Syntax:

Math.sqrt(value)

Example:

```
let number = 4;
let number1 = new String("400");
let string = "-20Mangos";
console.log(Math.sqrt(number));
console.log(Math.sqrt(number1));
console.log(Math.sqrt(string));
//output:
//2
//20
//NaN
```

cbrt():

It returns the cube root of the given value if it is convertible to a number else return NaN.

Syntax:

Math.cbrt(value)

Example:

```
let number = 8;
let string1 = new String("-64");
let string2 = "-8S";
console.log(Math.cbrt(number));
console.log(Math.cbrt(string1));
console.log(Math.cbrt(string2));
//output:
//2
//-4
//NaN
```

trunc():

It returns an integer part of the given value if it is convertible to a number else return NaN.

Syntax:

Math.trunc(value)

Example:

```
let number = 8.6767;
let string1 = new String("-64.78787");
let string2 = "-8S";
console.log(Math.trunc(number));
console.log(Math.trunc(string1));
console.log(Math.trunc(string2));
//output:
//8
//-64
//NaN
```

hypot():

It returns square root of sum of the squares of given values if all values are convertible to numbers else returns NaN.

Syntax:

Math.hypot(val1, val2,..., valN)

Example:

```
let number = 3;
let string1 = new String("-4");
let string2 = "-8S";
console.log(Math.hypot(number, string1));
console.log(Math.hypot(string1, string2));
//output:
//5
//NaN
```

log():

It returns natural logarithm of a given value if it is positive and convertible to a number else return NaN.

Syntax:

Math.log(value)

Example:

```
let number = 3;
let string1 = new String("4");
let string2 = "-8";
console.log(Math.log(number));
console.log(Math.log(string1));
console.log(Math.log(string2));
//output:
//1.0986122886681096
//1.3862943611198906
//NaN
```

sign():

It returns the sign of the given value if it is convertible to a number else return NaN.

Syntax:

Math.sign(vaule)

Example:

```
let number = 3;
let string1 = new String("-30");
let string2 = "-8s";
console.log(Math.sign(number));
console.log(Math.sign(string1));
console.log(Math.sign(string2));
//output:
//1
//-1
//NaN
```

sin():

It returns the sine of the given value if it is convertible to a number else return NaN.

Syntax:

Math.sin(value)

Example:

```
let number = 3;
let string1 = new String("-30");
let string2 = "-8s";
console.log(Math.sin(number));
console.log(Math.sin(string1));
console.log(Math.sin(string2));
//output:
//0.1411200080598672
//0.9880316240928618
//NaN
```

sinh():

It returns the hyperbolic sine of the given value if it is convertible to a number else return NaN.

Syntax:

Math.sinh(value)

Example:

```
let number = 3;
let string1 = new String("-30");
let string2 = "-8s";
console.log(Math.sinh(number));
console.log(Math.sinh(string1));
console.log(Math.sinh(string2));
//output:
//10.017874927409903
//-5343237290762.231
//NaN
```

cos():

It returns the cosine of the given value if it is convertible to a number else return NaN.

Syntax:

Math.cos(value)

Example:

```
let number = 3;
let string1 = new String("-30");
let string2 = "-8s";
console.log(Math.cos(number));
console.log(Math.cos(string1));
console.log(Math.cos(string2));
//output:
//-0.9899924966004454
//0.15425144988758405
//NaN
```

cosh():

It returns the hyperbolic cosine of the given value if it is convertible to a number else return NaN.

Syntax:

```
Math.cosh(value)
Example:
let number = 3;
let string1 = new String("-30");
let string2 = "-8s";
console.log(Math.cosh(number));
console.log(Math.cosh(string1));
console.log(Math.cosh(string2));
//output:
//10.067661995777765
//5343237290762.231
//NaN
```

tan():

It returns the tangent of the given value if it is convertible to a number else return NaN.

Syntax:

Math.tan(value)

Example:

```
let number = 3;
let string1 = new String("-30");
let string2 = "-8s";
console.log(Math.tan(number));
console.log(Math.tan(string1));
console.log(Math.tan(string2));
//output:
//-0.1425465430742778
//6.405331196646276
//NaN
```

tanh():

It returns the hyperbolic tangent of the given value if it is convertible to a number else return NaN.

Syntax:

Math.tanh(value)

Example:

```
let number = 45;
let string1 = new String("-30");
let string2 = "-8s";
console.log(Math.tanh(number));
console.log(Math.tanh(string1));
console.log(Math.tanh(string2));
//output:
//1
//-1
//NaN
```

acos():

It returns the arccosine of the given value in radians if value is convertible to number and between 0 to 1 else return NaN.

Syntax:

Math.acos(value)

Example:

```javascript
let number = 1;
let string1 = new String("-1");
let string2 = "1.2";
console.log(Math.acos(number));
console.log(Math.acos(string1));
console.log(Math.acos(string2));
//output:
//0
//3.141592653589793
//NaN
```

asin():

It returns the arcsine of the given value in radians if value is convertible to number and between 0 to 1 else return NaN.

Syntax:

Math.asin(value)

Example:

```javascript
let number = 1;
let string1 = new String("-1");
let string2 = "1.2";
console.log(Math.asin(number));
console.log(Math.asin(string1));
console.log(Math.asin(string2));
//output:
//1.5707963267948966
//-1.5707963267948966
//NaN
```

atan():

It returns the arc-tangent of the given value in radians if value is convertible to number else return NaN.

Syntax:

Math.atan(value)

Example:

```javascript
let number = 123123;
let string1 = new String("-64");
let string2 = "8s";
console.log(Math.atan(number));
console.log(Math.atan(string1));
console.log(Math.atan(string2));
//output:
//1.5707882048355553
//-1.5551725981744198
//NaN
```

JavaScript boolean object:

The **Boolean** object is used to represent two states either true or false.

Please note this is different from primitive Boolean. Any value assign to a Boolean object evaluates to true when it passes to conditional statement.

Example:

```javascript
const isTrue = new Boolean(false);
if (isTrue) {
    console.log('Yes, I am here.')
}
//output: Yes, I am here.
```

Please note, don't use Boolean constructor with new keyword to convert any value to Boolean. If you will use new keyword then it will return as an object.

Example:

```
const str = "Hello!";
const ok = Boolean(str);     // use this
const ok1 = !!(str);         // or this
const notOk = new Boolean(str); // don't use this!
console.log(ok)
console.log(ok1)
console.log(notOk)
//output:
//true
//true
//[Boolean: true]
```

Note: Boolean turns undefined, null, NaN, 0(zero), -0 (zero) and 0n to false and all others to true.

Below are two methods of Boolean object:

valueOf():

It returns the primitive value of Boolean object.

Syntax:

boolean.valueOf()

Example:

```
const boolNoParam = new Boolean();
const boolZero = new Boolean(1);
console.log(boolNoParam.valueOf())
console.log(boolZero.valueOf())
//output:
//false
//true
```

ToString():

It returns the string true/false based on the Boolean object value.

Syntax:

boolean.toString()

Example:

```
const boolNoParam = new Boolean();
const boolZero = new Boolean(1);
console.log(boolNoParam.toString(), typeof boolNoParam.toString())
console.log(boolZero.toString(), typeof boolZero.toString())
//output:
//false string
//true string
```

JavaScript RegExp Object:

a) Regular expressions are patterns used to match a combination of characters in strings.

b) We can write RegExp with in slashes /****/ or new keyword

```
const myReg = /db/g;
const matchedArr = 'bdbghdbbd'.match(myReg);
console.log(matchedArr);
//output:[ 'db', 'db' ]
```

using new key word

```
const myReg = new RegExp('db', 'g');
const matchedArr = 'bdbghdbbd'.match(myReg);
console.log(matchedArr);
//output:[ 'db', 'db' ]
```

Please note, in above examples '**g**' is a flag to search which enables global search. Below is the example without '**g**' flag.

```
const myReg = /db/;
const matchedArr = 'bdbghdbbd'.match(myReg);
console.log(matchedArr);
//output:[ 'db', index: 1, input: 'bdbghdbbd', groups: undefined ]
```

Some other important flags:

Flag	Description
d	Generate indices for substring matches.
g	Global search.

i	Case-insensitive search.
m	Allows ^ and $ to match newline characters.
s	Allows to match newline characters.

JavaScript Date Object:

JavaScript **Date** objects allow a developer to get datetime and perform the many different operations on it as per requirement. Date object returns datetime in a platform-independent format or in UTC.

Example:

```
let date = new Date();
console.log(date);// logs current UTC datatime
```

There are below constructors to create Date object:

```
new Date()
new Date(milliseconds)
new Date(date string)
new Date(year, month)
new Date(year, month, day)
new Date(year, month, day, hours)
new Date(year, month, day, hours, minutes)
new Date(year, month, day, hours, minutes, seconds)
new Date(year, month, day, hours, minutes, seconds, ms)
```

Some important methods to work with Date object:

getFullYear():

This method returns **year** as a four-digit number (yyyy).

Example

```
let date = new Date("2021-03-25T12:12:12.007Z");
console.log(date.getFullYear()); //2021
```

setFullYear():

This method uses to set the year.

Example

```
let date = new Date("2021-03-25T12:56:52.007Z");
date.setFullYear(2022);
console.log(date); //2022-03-25T12:56:52.007Z
```

getMonth():

This method returns **month** as a number (0-11).

Example

```
let date = new Date("2021-03-25T12:12:12.007Z");
console.log(date.getMonth()); //2
```

setMonth():

This method uses to set the month as a number (0-11).

Example

```
let date = new Date("2021-03-25T12:56:52.007Z");
date.setMonth(5);
console.log(date); //2021-06-25T12:56:52.007Z
```

getDate():

This method returns **day** as a number (1-31).

Example

```
let date = new Date("2021-03-25T12:12:12.007Z");
console.log(date.getDate()); //25
```

setDate():

This method uses to set **day** as a number (1-31).

Example

```
let date = new Date("2021-03-25T12:56:52.007Z");
date.setDate(15);
console.log(date); //2021-03-15T12:56:52.007Z
```

getDay():

This method returns **weekday** as a number (0-6).

Example

```
let date = new Date("2021-03-25T12:12:12.007Z");
console.log(date.getDay()); //4
```

getHours():

This method returns **hour** (0-23).

Example

```
let date = new Date("2021-03-25T12:12:12.007Z");
console.log(date.getHours()); //12
```

setHours():

This method uses to set **hour** (0-23).

Example

```
let date = new Date("2021-03-25T12:56:52.007Z");
date.setHours(4);
```

getMinutes():

This method returns **minute** (0-59).

Example

```
let date = new Date("2021-03-25T12:56:52.007Z");
console.log(date.getMinutes()); //56
```

setMinutes():

This method uses to set **minute** (0-59).

Example

```
let date = new Date("2021-03-25T12:56:52.007Z");
date.setMinutes(40);
console.log(date); //2021-03-25T12:40:52.007Z
```

getSeconds():

This method returns **second** (0-59).

Example

```
let date = new Date("2021-03-25T12:56:52.007Z");
console.log(date.getSeconds()); //52
```

setSeconds():

This method uses to set **second** (0-59).

Example

```
let date = new Date("2021-03-25T12:56:52.007Z");
date.setSeconds(40);
console.log(date); //2021-03-25T12:56:40.007Z
```

getMilliseconds():

This method returns **millisecond** (0-999).

Example

```
```

```
let date = new Date("2021-03-25T12:56:52.007Z");
console.log(date.getMilliseconds()); //7
```

setMilliseconds():

This method uses to set **millisecond** (0-999).

Example

```
let date = new Date("2021-03-25T12:56:52.007Z");
date.setMilliseconds(78);
console.log(date); //2021-03-25T12:56:52.078Z
```

getTime():

This method returns **time** (milliseconds since 1-jan-1970).

Example

```
let date = new Date("2021-03-25T12:56:52.007Z");
console.log(date.getTime()); //1616677012007
```

setTime():

This method uses to set **time** (milliseconds since 1-jan-1970).

Example

```
let date = new Date();
date.setTime(1616677012007);
console.log(date); //2021-03-25T12:56:52.007Z
```

Format dates:

Formatting dates depends on our requirement. In some countries, the month comes before the day followed by the year (2-26-2022). In others, the day comes before the month followed by the year (26-2-2022), and lots more.

This is not possible directly in JavaScript but we can achieve this using JavaScript date methods as below:

```
let date = new Date("2022-03-25");
let month = date.getMonth();
let day = date.getDate() + 1;
let year = date.getFullYear();
let format1 = `${month}/${day}/${year}`;
console.log(format1); // 2/26/2022
let format2 = `${day}/${month}/${year}`;
console.log(format2); // 26/2/2022
let format3 = `${month}-${day}-${year}`;
console.log(format3); // 2-26-2022
let format4 = `${day}-${month}-${year}`;
console.log(format4); // 26-2-2022
```

Note: we can achieve the same using **moment.js** very quickly and in better way. But we are not going to explain **moment.js** here because this is not part of core JavaScript date object.

JavaScript Set object:

The JavaScript Set object is used to store the **unique values of any type**, whether primitive values or object references. It automatically removes the duplicates.

It takes an iterable object as parameter and uses the concept of keys internally.

Example:

```
let sets = new Set([1000, 2000, 1000, 2000]);
console.log(sets);
// Output: Set { 1000, 2000 }
```

Below are some important methods of set object:

add():

It adds the specified values to the Set object.

Syntax:

set.add(element/value)

Example:

```
let sets = new Set([1000, 2000, 1000]);
sets.add(4000);
console.log(sets);
// Output: Set { 1000, 2000, 4000 }
```

delete():

It deletes the specified element from the Set object and then return true else return false if specified element not found in set.

Syntax:

set.delete(element/value)

Example:

```
let sets = new Set([1000, 2000, 1000]);
let isDeleted = sets.delete(1000);
console.log(isDeleted);
console.log(sets);
// Output:
// true
// Set { 2000 }
```

entries():

It returns an object of Set iterator that contains an array of [value, value] for each element.

Syntax:

set.entries()

Example:

```
let sets = new Set([1000, 2000, 1000]);
let entries = sets.entries();
for (let entry of entries)
    console.log(entry);
// Output:
// [ 1000, 1000 ]
// [ 2000, 2000 ]
```

values():

It returns an object of Set iterator that contains the values for each element.

Syntax:

set.values()

Example:

```
let sets = new Set([1000, 2000, 1000]);
let values = sets.values();
for (let value of values)
    console.log(value);
// Output:
// 1000
// 2000
```

clear():

It clears the Set object.

Syntax:

set.clear()

Example:

```
let sets = new Set([1000, 2000, 1000]);
console.log(sets);
sets.clear();
console.log(sets);
// Output:
// Set { 1000, 2000 }
// Set {}
```

forEach():

It executes the function specified with in forEach() method once for each value.

Example:

```
let sets = new Set([1000, 2000, 1000]);
sets.forEach((ele, index, sets) => {
    console.log(ele, ',', index, ',', sets);
})
// Output:
// 1000 , 1000 , Set { 1000, 2000 }
// 2000 , 2000 , Set { 1000, 2000 }
```

has():

It returns true if the Set object contains the specified value element else returns false.

Syntax:

set.has(element/value)

Example:

```
let sets = new Set([1000, 2000, 1000]);
console.log(sets.has(1000))
console.log(sets.has(3000))
// Output:
// true
// false
```

JavaScript Map object:

JavaScript Map object is used to store key-value pairs and remembers the original insertion order of the keys. Any type of value (primitives or object) may be used for either a key or a value.

A Map object cannot contain duplicate keys but values can be duplicate.

Example:

```
let map = new Map([
    ["Key1", "value1"],
    ["Key2", "value2"],
]);
console.log(map);
//output: Map { 'Key1' => 'value1', 'Key2' => 'value2' }
```

Below are some important methods of Map object:

set():

It adds the key-value pairs to Map object or update value if the given key already exists.

Syntax:

Map.set(key,value)

Example:

```
let map = new Map();
map.set("key1", "value1");
map.set("key2", "value2");
map.set("key1", "value3");
console.log(map);
//output: Map { 'key1' => 'value3', 'key2' => 'value2' }
```

get():

It returns the value of specified key.

Syntax:

Map.get(key)

Example:

```
let map = new Map();
map.set("key1", "value1");
map.set("key2", "value2");
console.log(map.get("key2"));
//output: value2
```

has():

It returns true if the map object contains the specified key otherwise returns false.

Syntax:

Map.has(key)

Example:

```
let map = new Map();
map.set("key1","value1");
map.set("key2","value2");
console.log(map.has("key2"));
console.log(map.has("key3"));
//output:
//true
//false
```

keys():

It returns all the keys as Map iterator.

Syntax:

map.keys()

Example:

```
let map = new Map([["oranges",50],["bananas",100]]);
let keys = map.keys();
console.log(keys);
for(let key of keys)
console.log(key)
//output:
//[Map Iterator] { 'oranges', 'bananas' }
//oranges
//bananas
```

values():

It returns all the values as Map iterator.

Syntax:

map.values()

Example:

```
let map = new Map([["oranges",50],["bananas",100]]);
let values = map.values();
console.log(values);
for(let value of values)
console.log(value)
//output:
//[Map Iterator] { 50, 100 }
//50
//100
```

clear():

It clears Map object or removes all elements.

Syntax:

map.clear()

Example:

```
let map = new Map([["oranges",50],["bananas",100]]);
console.log(map);
map.clear();
console.log(map);
//output:
//Map { 'oranges' => 50, 'bananas' => 100 }
//Map {}
```

delete():

It deletes the element based on the specified key from a Map object. It returns true if key exists and element deleted else return false.

Syntax:

map.delete(key)

Example:

```
let map = new Map([["oranges",50],["bananas",100]]);
console.log(map);
let isDeleted = map.delete("oranges");
console.log(isDeleted)
console.log(map);
//output:
//Map { 'oranges' => 50, 'bananas' => 100 }
//true
//Map { 'bananas' => 100 }
```

entries():

It returns an object of Map iterator that contains all key-value pair.

Syntax:

map.entries()

Example:

```
let map = new Map([["oranges",50],["bananas",100]]);
let entries = map.entries();
console.log(map);
for(let entry of entries)
console.log(entry)
//output:
//Map { 'oranges' => 50, 'bananas' => 100 }
//[ 'oranges', 50 ]
//[ 'bananas', 100 ]
```

forEach():

It executes the specified function once for each key/value pair.

Example:

```
let map = new Map([["oranges",50],["bananas",100]]);
map.forEach((key,value,map)=>{
    console.log(key,value);
})
//output:
//50 oranges
//100 bananas
```

Prototype in JavaScript

The prototype provides flexibility to add new properties to an object at any time.

The prototype is a property of type object that is associated to every function and object by default.

Any property added using prototype object is shared with all instances of its constructor function.

Let's discuss an example for better understanding.

Suppose you have a function named 'person' with two properties 'firstName' and 'lastName', later you want to add a function named 'getFullName' which will return 'firstName + lastName'.

Below are the ways to implement this requirement.

1. Adding getFullName to every created object.

2. Adding getFullName to prototype

Adding getFullName to every created object.

```javascript
function person(firstName, lastName) {
    this.firstName = firstName;
    this.lastName = lastName;
}


let p1 = new person("john", "petro");
let p2 = new person("Jammy", "Kendo");


console.log(`p1(firstName: ${p1.firstName}, lastName: ${p1.lastName})`);
//p1(firstName: john, lastName: petro)
console.log(`p2(firstName: ${p2.firstName}, lastName: ${p2.lastName})`);
//p2(firstName: Jammy, lastName: Kendo)


//adding getFullName
p1.getFullName = function () {
    return `${this.firstName} ${this.lastName}`
}


console.log(`p1(fullName: ${p1.getFullName()})`); //p1(fullName: john petro)
console.log(`p2(fullName: ${p2.getFullName()})`); //TypeError: p2.getFullName
is not a function
```

In above example, you can see p2.getFullName() throws **TypeError** because getFullName method only added on p1 not on p2 if you want access getFullName on p2 then you need to add the same on p2 which is not good.

So better to use 2nd way to achieve this type of requirement.

Adding getFullName to prototype

Let's add getFullName to prototype of function instead of object as below:

```javascript
function person(firstName, lastName) {
    this.firstName = firstName;
    this.lastName = lastName;
}


let p1 = new person("john", "petro");
let p2 = new person("Jammy", "Kendo");

console.log(`p1(firstName: ${p1.firstName}, lastName: ${p1.lastName})`);
//p1(firstName: john, lastName: petro)
console.log(`p2(firstName: ${p2.firstName}, lastName: ${p2.lastName})`);
//p2(firstName: Jammy, lastName: Kendo)

//adding getFullName
person.prototype.getFullName = function () {
    return `${this.firstName} ${this.lastName}`
}

console.log(`p1(fullName: ${p1.getFullName()})`); //p1(fullName: john petro)
console.log(`p2(fullName: ${p2.getFullName()})`); //p2(fullName: Jammy Kendo)
```

Now you can observe adding getFullName() in prototype works for all objects.

Note: You can access a prototype of an object using **__proto__** property of that object or

Object.getPrototypeOf() method.

Example:

```javascript
function person(firstName, lastName) {
    this.firstName = firstName;
    this.lastName = lastName;
}


let p1 = new person("john", "petro");
person.prototype.getFullName = function () {
    return this.firstName + this.lastName;
}
console.log(p1.__proto__); //person {getFullName: [Function]}
console.log(Object.getPrototypeOf(p1)); //person {getFullName: [Function]}
console.log(p1.__proto__ === Object.getPrototypeOf(p1)); //true
```

JavaScript Variables

A variable is a container for storing a value, like a number we might use in a sum or any other operation, or a string that we might use as part of a sentence or displaying to user.

For declaring a variable, we can use one of below keyword:

1. Var
2. Cosnt
3. Let

```
var title = "JavaScript";
console.log(title); //JavaScript

const BOOK_NAME = "JavaScript Basics";
console.log(BOOK_NAME); //JavaScript Basics

let subTitle = "JavaScript Data Types";
console.log(subTitle); //JavaScript Data Types
```

Important about Var:

a) At the time of JavaScript was created, this was the only way to declare variables. The design of var is confusing and error-prone.

b) We can update the value of Var variable.

c) if you write a multiline JavaScript program in which you can initialize a variable with a value before declare it with **var** keyword and it will still work.

```
name = "John";
function logName() {
    console.log(name);
}
logName();
var name;
//Output : John
```

Note: Above program works because of **JavaScript Hoisting** behavior/feature. We will read about JavaScript Hoisting in dept later.

Important about let:

a) The let keyword was introduced in ES6.

b) This is limited to the scope of block statement. Which means variable only works with bock where it declares.

```javascript
function logName() {
    {
        let name = "peter";
        console.log(name); //works fine
    }
    console.log(name); //gives error (outside scope)
}
logName();
//Output
//peter
//ReferenceError: name is not defined
```

c) We can update the value of let variable.

d) JavaScript hoisting no longer works with let.

Let's try to replace var with let in above example.

```javascript
name = "John";
function logName() {
    console.log(name);
}
logName();
let name;
//Output : ReferenceError: Cannot access 'name' before initialization
```

Important about const:

a) The const keyword was introduced in ES6.

b) This is limited to the scope of block statement. Same as let.

c) Const variable must be initialize at the time of declaration.

```javascript
const name = "john"; //same line declaration and initialization
```

Initialization in different line gives error:

```
const name;
name = "john";

//output: SyntaxError: Missing initializer in const declaration
```

d) JavaScript hoisting no longer works with const as well.

```
function logName() {
    console.log(name);
}
logName();
const name = "john";
//output: ReferenceError: Cannot access 'name' before initialization
```

e) We can't update the value of const variable

```
const name = "john";
function logName() {
    console.log(name);
    name = "peter"; //gives error here
}
logName();
//output:
//john
//TypeError: Assignment to constant variable.
```

JavaScript object and array destructuring:

The **destructuring assignment** is a good way to initialize distinct variables with the values from arrays, or properties from objects.

Array destructuring:

You have an array with 5 elements, you want to access 1st, 3rd and 5th elements from the same array then you can access the same as below:

```
let arr = [0, 1, 2, 3, 4];
console.log(arr[0]);   //0
console.log(arr[2]);   //2
console.log(arr[4]);   //4
```

But with the help of destructuring you can do the same as below:

```
let arr = [0, 1, 2, 3, 4];
let [var1, , var3, , var5] = arr;
console.log(var1); //0
console.log(var3); //2
console.log(var5); //4
```

If you want to assign some items of an array to variables and rest of items to a particular variable then you can do this as below:

```
let arr = [0, 1, 2, 3, 4];
let [var1, var2, ...restVar] = arr;
console.log(var1); //0
console.log(var2); //1
console.log(restVar); //[ 2, 3, 4 ]
```

You can also initialize variables with default value as below:

```
let arr = [, "I", "am", "John"];
let [greeting = "Hello", , , name = "Jack"] = arr;
console.log(greeting, name); //Hello John
```

Object destructuring:

Let's you have an object with lot of properties but you want to access only some properties then you can access the same as below:

```javascript
let person = {
    firstName: "John",
    lastName: "petro",
    address: {
        city: "Noida",
        country: "India"
    }
}

console.log(person.firstName); //john
console.log(person.lastName); //petro
console.log(person.address.city); //Noida
```

But with the help of destructuring you can do the same as below:

```javascript
let person = {
    firstName: "John",
    lastName: "petro",
    address: {
        city: "Noida",
        country: "India"
    }
}

let { firstName, lastName, address: { city } } = person;
console.log(firstName); //john
console.log(lastName); //petro
console.log(city); //Noida
```

If you want to assign some properties of an object to variables and rest of object to a particular variable then you can do this as below:

```
let person = {
    firstName: "John",
    lastName: "petro",
    address: {
        city: "Noida",
        country: "India"
    }
}

let { firstName, ...otherInfo } = person;
console.log(firstName); //john
console.log(otherInfo); //{ lastName: 'petro', address: { city: 'Noida',
country: 'India' } }
```

You can also initialize variables with default value as below:

```
let person = {
    lastName: "petro",
    address: {
        city: "Noida",
        country: "India"
    }
}

let { firstName = "John", lastName = "Peter", ...otherInfo } = person;
console.log(firstName, lastName); //john petro
console.log(otherInfo); //{ address: { city: 'Noida', country: 'India' } }
```

You can use different name for variables than properties name:

```
let person = {
    lastName: "petro",
    address: {
        city: "Noida",
        country: "India"
    }
}

let { firstName: fname = "John", lastName: lname, ...otherInfo } = person;
console.log(fname, lname); //john petro
console.log(otherInfo); //{ address: { city: 'Noida', country: 'India' } }
```

JavaScript Spread Operator:

The JavaScript spread (…) operator allows an iterable (array or string) to be expanded/appended in places where zero or more elements are expected.

Using the spread (…) operator we can easily achieve below things:

1. Copy an array to another
2. Expand one array with another
3. Concatenate two or more array
4. Convert an array to object using key and value pairs

Copy an array to another:

Using JavaScript spread (…) operator, it is very easy to create a copy of one array to another.

```
let arr = [1, 2, 3];
let copyArr = [...arr]; //copy array
arr.push(4); //this will not effect new array
copyArr.push("Hello"); //this will not effect old array
console.log(arr); //[ 1, 2, 3, 4 ]
console.log(copyArr); //[ 1, 2, 3, 'Hello' ]
```

Expand one array with another

The JavaScript spread (…) operator allows to append or expand one array with the help of another array.

```
let initialNumber = [1, 2, 3];
let numbers = [...initialNumber, 4, 5, 6];
console.log(numbers); //[ 1, 2, 3, 4, 5, 6 ]
```

Concatenate two or more array:

You can also concatenate two or more array with the help of spread (…) operator.

```
let arr = [1, 2, 3];
let arr1 = [4, 5, 6];
let mainArr = [...arr, ...arr1];
console.log(mainArr); // [ 1, 2, 3, 4, 5, 6 ]
```

Convert an array to object using key and value pairs

With the help of spread (…) operator, you can convert an array to an object (key/value pair)

```
let greetings = ["hello", 'hi', "good morning"];
let obj = { ...greetings };
console.log(obj); //{ '0': 'hello', '1': 'hi', '2': 'good morning' }
```

In case of object, the spread (…) object allows to enumerates the properties of one abject, to be appended in another object as key-value pairs.

1. Copy an object to another
2. Expand one object with another
5. Concatenate two or more objects

Copy an object to another:

Spread (…) operator is an easy way to create a new object based on another object or creating copy.

```
let person = {
    firstName: "John",
    address: {
        city: "Noida",
        country: "India"
    }
}

//create copy from person
let copyPerson = { ...person };

copyPerson.firstName = "James"; //This is simple propery so will not effect person
copyPerson.address.city = "Meerut"; //This will effect both

console.log(person); //{ firstName: 'John', address: { city: 'Meerut', country: 'India' } }
console.log(copyPerson); //{ firstName: 'James', address: { city: 'Meerut', country: 'India' } }
```

Expand one object with another

You can also append one object to another as below:

```javascript
let person = {
    firstName: "John",
    address: {
        city: "Noida",
        country: "India"
    }
}

//create object with appending person
let newPerson = { lastName: "Petro", ...person };

newPerson.firstName = "James"; //This is simple propery so will not effect person
newPerson.address.city = "Meerut"; //This will effect both

console.log(person); //{ firstName: 'John', address: { city: 'Meerut', country: 'India' } }
console.log(newPerson); //{ lastName: 'Petro', firstName: 'James', address: { city: 'Meerut', country: 'India' } }
```

Concatenate two or more objects:

Spread operator allows to concatenate two to more object's properties to one object.

```javascript
let personData = {
    firstName: "John",
    lastName: "Petro"
}

let addressData = {
    address: {
        city: "Noida",
        country: "India"
    }
}

//create one using above objects
let person = { ...personData, ...addressData };

console.log(person); //{ firstName: 'John', lastName: 'Petro', address: { city: 'Noida', country: 'India' } }
```

JavaScript Comments:

Comments are the most important feature of any programming language. Comments can be used to explain JavaScript code, and to make it more understandable or readable.

There are two types of comments in JavaScript:

Single line comments:

a) Single line comments start with // (Double slashes)

b) Anything written between // and the end of the line will not be executed or ignored by JavaScript interpreter

c)

Example:

```
//Declare a variable x and assign 5
let x = 5;
let y = x + 2;  // Declare y and assign a value (x + 2)
```

Multi line comments:

a) Multi line comments start with **/* (slash followed by an asterisk)** and end with ***/ (asterisk followed by a slash)**

b) Anything written between **/*** and ***/** will not be executed or ignored by JavaScript interpreter.

Example:

```
/* Declare a variable x and assign 5 */
let x = 5;
/* Declare y
and assign a value (x + 2) */
let y = x + 2;
```

JavaScript this Keyword:

In a very simple words, JavaScript this keyword holds the reference of an object. But it works a little differently in strict mode and non-strict mode.

In non–strict mode, this always holds a reference to an object.

Example:

```
const car = {
    type: "fiat",
    model: 500,
    getCarInfo: function () {
        return this.type + ' ' + this.model;
    }
};
console.log(car.getCarInfo());
//output: fiat 500
```

To identify the referenced object (which object is referred by this keyword), we need to understand deferent context of this keyword.

This keyword in function context:

If we are using this keyword inside a function then the value of this is the object that is used to call the function. In simple words, if the function is called using obj1.func(), then this refers to obj1.

Example:

```
function getReference() {
    return this;
}
const car = {
    type: "fiat",
    model: 500
}
car.getThis = getReference;

console.log(car.getThis());
  //output:{ type: 'fiat', model: 500, getThis: [Function: getReference]
```

If a function is called without any object, then this referred to **globalThis**.

```
function getReference() {
    return this;
}
console.log(getReference() === globalThis);
  //output: true
```

Please note, we can also explicitly set the reference value of this keyword using the call(), apply().

Example:

```
const obj = {
    getReference: function () {
        return this;
    }
}
const obj1 = { name: "obj1" }
console.log(obj.getReference.call(obj1));
console.log(obj.getReference.apply(obj1));
  //output:
  //{ name: 'obj1' }
  //{ name: 'obj1' }
```

Similar to call() and apply(), we can also use bind() method. Using bind() method, we can create a new method with specific value of this.

Example:

```
const obj = {
    getReference: function () {
        return this;
    }
}
const obj1 = { name: "obj1" };
const functionRef = obj.getReference.bind(obj1);
console.log(functionRef());
  //output:
  //{ name: 'obj1' }
```

This keyword in global context:

In the global context, outside of function or class. this keyword refers to the browser window object.

Example:

```
console.log(this === window); // true
```

JavaScript Hoisting:

The Hoisting is the default behavior of JavaScript. JavaScript interpreter moves all the declarations of variables, functions or classes at the top of their scope before code execution.

The advantage of hoisting is that no matter where variables and functions are declared, they are automatically moved at the top of their scope either their scope is global or local.

Variable hoisting:

var-declared variables support hoisting, meaning all the declarations of var-declared variables are moved at the top their scope (function or global). If you try to access a variable before it's declaration, the value always returns 'undefined'.

Example:

1. Function scope variables:

```
function print() {
    console.log(a);
    var a = 10;
}
print();
//output:
//undefined
```

2. Global scope variable:

```
console.log(a);
var a = 10;
//output:
//undefined
```

Please note, JavaScript hoisting only moves declarations at top of their scope, not initializations. So, the above example is interpreted as:

1. Function scope variables:

```javascript
function print() {
    var a;
    console.log(a);
    a = 10;
}
print();
//output:
//undefined
```

2. Global scope variables:

```javascript
var a;
console.log(a);
a = 10;
//output:
//undefined
```

Please note, let and const declared variables are block level variable and they don't support hoisting.

Below example gives reference error because we are using let and const declared variables.

Example:

```javascript
console.log(let_a);
let let_a = 10;
//output:
//ReferenceError: Cannot access 'let_a' before initialization
```

Function hoisting:

Function hoisting is similar to variable hoisting, meaning JavaScript interpreter moves the entire function declaration to the top of their scope. If you try to call a function before it's declaration, then the function code runs without any error.

Example:

```
print();
function print() {
    console.log("Hello! I am a function.")
}
//output:
//Hello! I am a function.
```

the code above is equivalent to:

```
function print() {
    console.log("Hello! I am a function.")
}
print();
  //output:
  //Hello! I am a function.
```

Please note, the function literals don't support hoisting. Below example gives type error.

```
print();
var print = function () {
    console.log("Hello! I am a function.")
}
//output:
//TypeError: print is not a function
```

JavaScript Console API methods:

A set of methods provide by the Console API is very useful while developing a JavaScript/web application. which provides functionality to allow developers to perform debugging tasks, such as logging messages, errors, warning or the values of variables in your code, or time taken by an operation to complete.

Here we will explain some important methods out of all these:

Console.log() : method returns a message to the web console. The message may be a single line, or any one or more JavaScript objects.

```
console.log(str, object1)
console.log(str, object1, /* ..., */ objectN)
```

Console.debug() : method returns a message to the web console at the "debug" log level.

```
console.debug(str, object1)
console.debug(str, object1, /* …, */ objectN)
```

Console.Assert(): method returns an error message to the console if the assertion condition is calculated false else nothing happens.

```
console.assert(5 % 2 === 0, "this is not", "an even number");
//output: Assertion failed: this is not an even number
```

Console.Error(): method returns an error message to the Web console in red color.

```
console.error("hello");
//output : hello
```

Console.Count(): method returns the number of times that this count() has been called.

```
console.count();  //default : 1
console.count(); //default : 2
```

Console.ResetCount(): method resets counter used with console.count() method.

```
console.count();  //default: 1
console.count(); //default: 2
console.countReset() //this will reset count value
console.count() //default: 1
```

Console.Time() : method starts a timer

Console.timeLog() : method returns the current value of a timer that was previously started using console.time().

Console.timeEnd(): method stops a timer that was previously started using console.time().

Example:

```
console.time();  //this starts a timer
console.timeLog(); //this logs the current value of timer
console.timeEnd(); /*this logs the value of timer taken between console.time()
and console.timeEnd() and then stop the timer*/
console.timeLog(); //logs a waring because no timer alive now
console.timeEnd(); //logs a warning because no timer alive now
```

Operators in JavaScript:

We (all) are familiar with operators. So here we are not going to explain operators in details just giving you overview about the operators and their uses with example.

There are different types of JavaScript operators:

Arithmetic Operators: are used to perform arithmetic operations on numbers. Below are some important Arithmetic operators.

Operator	Example	Result
+ (Addition)	let res = 5 + 2;	7
- (Subtraction)	let res = 5 - 2;	3
* (Multiplication)	let res = 5 * 2;	10
/ (Division)	let res = 5 / 2;	2.5
++ (Increment)	let num = 5; let res = ++num;	6
-- (Decrement)	let num = 5; let res = --num;	4
% (Modulus)	let res = 5 % 2;	1

Assignment Operators: are used to assign values to JavaScript variables. Below are some examples of assignment operators.

Operator	Example	Simple form
=	A = B	A = B
+=	A += B	A = A + B
- =	A -= B	A = A - B
*=	A *= B	A = A * B
/=	A /= B	A = A / B
%=	A %= B	A = A % B

Comparison Operators: are used to compare its operands/values and returns a logical value based on whether the comparison is true. The operands can be numerical, string, logical, or object values. Below are some comparison operators.

Operator	Example	Result
== (Equal)	5 == '5'	True
!= (not equal)	5 != '5'	False
=== (Strict equal)	5 === '5'	False
!== (Strict not equal)	5 !== '5'	True
> (Greater than)	5 > 5	False
>= (Greater than equal)	5 >= 5	True
< (Less than)	5 < 5	False
<= (Less than equal)	5 <= 5	True

Logical Operators: are uses with one or two operands' and returns a logical value. Below are the important logical operators.

Operator	Usage	Description	Important
&& (Logical AND)	exp1 && exp2	Returns true if both operands are true; otherwise, returns false.	Returns exp1 if it can be converted to false; otherwise, returns exp2. Ex: 0 && 7 //Result = 0 5 && 7 //Result = 7
|| (Logical OR)	exp1 || exp2	Returns true if either operand is true; if both are false, returns false.	Returns exp1 if it can be converted to true; otherwise, returns exp2. Ex: 0 && 7 //Result = 7 5 && 7 //Result = 5
! (Logical NOT)	!exp	Returns false if its single operand that can be converted to true; otherwise, returns true.	Ex: !0 //Result = true !5 //Result = false

Conditional Operators: is also known as Ternary operator. if a specified condition is truthy returns one value/expression else return another if it is false.

Example:

```
let num = 10;
let msg = num % 2 === 0 ? "Number is even." : "Number is odd.";
console.log(msg); //Number is even.
```

Type Operators: are used to identify the type of operand

Operator	Description	Example // Result
Typeof	Returns the type of a variable	typeof 5 // number typeof 'JavaScript' //string
instanceof	Returns true if an object is an instance of an object type	let num = new Number(5); num instanceof Number //true

Bitwise Operators: Bitwise operators are also known as Binary operators. These operators treat its operands as a set of 32-bit binary digits (zeros and ones) to perform the action. But the result is display as a decimal value. Below are the Bitwise operators:

Operator	Description	Example //result	Internal representation //result
&(AND)	Return each bit to 1 if both bits are 1	5 & 1 //1	0101 & 0001 //0001
|(OR)	Return each bit to 1 if one of two bits is 1	5 | 1 //5	0101 | 0001 //0101
^(XOR)	Return each bit to 1 if only one of two bits is 1	5 ^ 1 //4	0101 ^ 0001 //0100
<<(Zero fill left shift)	Shifts left by adding zeros from the right	5 << 2 //20	0101 << 2 //010100

>>(Signed right shift)	Shifts right by adding copies of the leftmost bit from the left	5 >> 2 //1	0101 >> 2 //0001
>>>(Zero fill right shift)	Shifts right by adding zeros from the left	5 >>> 2 //1	0101 >>> 2 //0001
~(NOT)	Inverts each bit	~5 //-6	~00000000000000000000000000000101 //11111111111111111111111111111010

Please note, A signed integer uses the leftmost bit as the minus sign.

```
00000000000000000000000000000101(5)
11111111111111111111111111111010(~5 = -6)
```

Conditions or decisions making in your code:

In any programming language, we need to implement decisions and choose an action accordingly based on different inputs.

For example, a person has completed his 18th year can vote other he cannot vote.

So, in above example age is condition based on that we can say he can vote or cannot.

For achieving the same, JavaScript has conditional statements which allow us to represent such decision making in our program.

1. If...else statement
2. If...else if...else statement
3. Switch statement
4. Ternary statement or operator

If...else statement

The **if...else** statement executes if clause if a specified condition is truthy. If the condition is falsy, then else clause will be executed.

Syntax:

```
if (condition) {
    //code to run if condition is truthy
}
else {
    //run code instead
}
```

Below example allows a person to vote only if he has completed his 18th year.

```
let age = 19;
if (age > 18) {
    console.log("He/She can vote.");
}
else {
    console.log("He/She can't vote.");
}
//output: He/She can vote.
```

Please note, in above statement else part is optional either you can use or not. This depends on the requirement.

```
let age = 19;
if (age > 18) {
    console.log("He/She can vote.");
}
//output: He/She can vote.
```

If...else if...else statement

The **if...else if...else** statement is similar to **if...else** statement. However, we can handle multiple if statements using **if...else if...else.** This checks the if clause one by one and executes an if clause if a specified condition is truthy. If the condition is falsy, then next if clause condition will be check and so on.

Syntax:

```
if (condition) {
    //code to run if condition is truthy otherwise check next else if
condition
}
else if (condition) {
    //code to run if condition is truthy otherwise check next else if
condition
    //if not present then executes else condition
}
else {
    //run code instead
}
```

Example:

```
let number = 10;
if (number < 0) {
    console.log("Number is negative.");
}
else if (number > 0) {
    console.log("Number is positive.");
}
else {
    console.log("Number is Zero(0).");
}
//output : Number is positive.
```

Note:

1. **Else** statement is optional same as if...else statement. **But this is not a good practice to use if...else if...else statement without else.**

```
let number = 10;
if (number < 0) {
    console.log("Number is negative.");
}
else if (number > 0) {
    console.log("Number is positive.");
}
//output : Number is positive.
```

2. We can also use if...else or if...else if...else statement with in another if, else if or else statement.

```javascript
let number = 10;
if (number < 0) {
    console.log("Number is negative.");
}
else if (number > 0) {
    if (number < 10) {
        console.log("Number has single digit.");
    }
    else {
        console.log("Number has two or more digits.");
    }
}
else {
    console.log("Number is Zero(0).");
}
//output : Number has two or more digits.
```

Switch statement

if...else statements are good enough to enabling conditional code well, but they have some downsides. They are mainly good where you have a couple of choices, and each choice requires a group of code lines/statements or a reasonable amount of code to be run, and/or the conditions are complex.

But when you just want to set a variable or execute a small code depending on a condition, the syntax can be a bit cumbersome, especially if you have a large number of conditions/choices. In these cases, the switch statement is better than if...else statements.

Switch statement follows below point.

1. Started with switch keyword, followed by a set of parentheses.

2. A value of expression within the parentheses.

3. The keyword case, followed by a choice, followed by a colon (:).

4. Some code lines to run if the choice matches the expression/value.

5. A break statement, followed by a semicolon. If the choice matches the expression/value given with in switch parenthesis, the browser stops executing the switch block here, and moves on to the code line that appears below the switch statement.

6. You can write many other cases (point 3-5) based on the requirements

7. The keyword default, followed by exactly the same code pattern as one of the cases (point 3–5) without choice after it, and no break statement needed. Because this is last in the block and it runs only if none of the choices match.

Syntax:

```
switch (expression / value) {
    case choise1:
        //code to run
        break;
    case choise2:
        //code to run
        break;

    //incluse as many cases

    default:
    //code to run if no choice matches
}
```

Example:

```
let num = 15;
switch (parseInt(num / 10)) {
    case 0:
        console.log("Numebr is b/w 0-9.");
        break;
    case 1:
        console.log("Numebr is b/w 10-19.");
        break;
    case 2:
        console.log("Numebr is b/w 20-29.");
        break;
    default:
        console.log("Numebr is greater than 29.");
}

//output: Numebr is b/w 10-19.
```

Please note, if the keyword **break** or **return** is not existed with in a case then the code of subsequent cases will execute till the break or return keyword not found or till the default case.

```
let num = 15;
switch (parseInt(num / 10)) {
    case 0:
        console.log("Numebr is b/w 0-9.");
        break;
    case 1:
        console.log("Numebr is b/w 10-19."); //no break exist
    case 2:
        console.log("Numebr is b/w 20-29.");
        break;
    default:
        console.log("Numebr is greater than 29.");
}

//output:
//Numebr is b/w 10-19.
//Numebr is b/w 20-29.
```

Ternary operator/statement

Ternary operator is also works as condition statement. if a specified condition is truthy returns one value/expression else return another if it is false.

Syntax:

```
condition ? run this code if condition is truthy: else run this code
```

Example:

```
let num = 10;
let msg = num % 10 === 0 ? "Number is even." : "Number is odd.";
console.log(msg);
//output: Number is even.
```

Loop and Iterations:

The JavaScript loops are a way to iterate a set of statements or a code block repeatedly.

Below are the various iteration statements available in JavaScript.

1. while statement
2. do...while statement
3. for statement

4. labeled statement

5. break statement

6. continue statement

7. for...of statement

8. for...in statement

while statement:

A while statement runs its code/statements as long as given condition evaluates to true else code execution starts from the next line after while statement.

A while statement declares as:

```
while (conditional expression)
{
    //statements
}
```

The condition test evaluated *before* the statements inside the loop is executed. If the condition evaluates true, statements are executed and the condition is evaluated again. If the condition evaluates false then the statement execution stops, and control is passed to the next statement after **while** statement.

To execute multiple statements inside while, use all the statements with in { } (curly braces).

Example:

```
let n = 0;
let str = "";
while (n < 10) {
    n++;
    str += 2 * n + ",";
}
console.log(str);

//output:
//2,4,6,8,10,12,14,16,18,20,
```

Explanation: in the above example for each iteration,

1. first loop evaluates the condition n < 10 if it's true go to step 2.

2. The loop increments n by 1 and multiply that value to 2 and then assign to a variable

116

3. Repeat the point 1-2 until the condition of loop evaluates false.

do...while statement:

A **do...while** statement runs its code/statements as long as given condition evaluates to true else code execution starts from the next line after **do...while** statement same as while.

But in **do...while** statement, first executes the statements and then evaluates the condition. Which means the statements inside **do...while** loop executes before and then do the condition check.

A do...while statement declares as:

```
do {
    //statements
} while (conditional expression)
```

The statements inside the loop executed *before* the condition test evaluated. If the condition evaluates true, statements are executed again. If the condition evaluates false then the statement execution stops, and control is passed to the next statement after **do...while** statement.

To execute multiple statements inside do...while, use all the statements with in { } (curly braces).

Example:

```
let i = 2;
let n = 0;
let str = "";
do {
    n++;
    str += 2 * n + ",";
} while (n < 10)
console.log(str);
//output:
//2,4,6,8,10,12,14,16,18,20,
```

Explanation: in the above example for each iteration,

1. First loop increments n by 1 and multiply that value to 2 and then assign to a variable
2. Then loop evaluates the condition n < 10 if it's true go to step 1.
3. Repeat the point 1-2 until the condition of loop evaluates false.

for statement:

A **for** statement runs its code/statements as long as given condition evaluates to true else code execution starts from the next line after **for** statement.

A for statement declares as:

```
for (initialization; conditionalExpression; afterthought) {
    //statements
}
```

for loop uses below steps to execute:

1. The initialization expression usually initializes loop counter variables. Using initialization expression, we can also declare variables.

2. The conditional expression is evaluated If the condition evaluates true, statements are executed. If the condition evaluates false then the statement execution stops, and control is passed to the next statement after **for** statement.

3. If afterthought expression is executed if its present.

4. Control goes to Step 2 again.

Example:

```
let str = "";
for (let n = 1; n <= 10; n++) {
    str += 2 * n + ",";
}
console.log(str);
//output:
//2,4,6,8,10,12,14,16,18,20,
```

labeled statement:

A label **statement** uses to provide a statement with an identifier. Later in your program use can use this label to refer the specified code.

Example:

```
let str = "";
forLoop: for (let n = 1; n <= 10; n++) {
    str += 2 * n + ",";
}
console.log(str);
//output:
//2,4,6,8,10,12,14,16,18,20,
```

Please note, how can we use this labeled statement? Please read break and continue statements.

break statement:

The break statement is used to terminate the loop statements (while, do...while and for) based on some specific condition. If you are using multiple loop statements one inside another. The break terminates the innermost enclosing loop.

Example:

```
for (let i = 1; i < 3; i++) {
    let str = "";
    for (let n = 1; n <= 10; n++) {
        str += i * n + ",";
        if (n === 5)
            break;
    }
    console.log(str);
}
//output:
//1,2,3,4,5,
//2,4,6,8,10,
```

break statement with labeled statement:

```
outerLoop: for (let i = 1; i < 3; i++) {
    innerLoop: for (let n = 1; n <= 10; n++) {
        console.log(i * n);
        if (n === 5)
            break outerLoop; //break using outerLoop labeled statement
    }
}
//output:
//1
//2
//3
//4
//5
```

continue statement:

The continue statement is used to terminates the current iteration of loop statements (while, do...while and for) based on some specific condition. If you are using multiple loop statements one inside another. The continue terminates the current iteration of innermost enclosing loop.

Example:

```
for (let i = 1; i < 3; i++) {
    let str = "";
    for (let n = 1; n <= 10; n++) {
        str += i * n + ",";
        if (n === 5) {
            console.log(str);
            continue;
        }
    }
    console.log("end outer loop", i);
}

//output:
//1,2,3,4,5,
//end outer loop 1
//2,4,6,8,10,
//end outer loop 2
```

continue statetment with labeled statement:

```javascript
outerLoop: for (let i = 1; i < 3; i++) {
    let str = "";
    innerLoop: for (let n = 1; n <= 10; n++) {
        str += i * n + ",";
        if (n === 5) {
            console.log(str);
            continue outerLoop; //continue using outerLoop labeled statement
        }
    }
    console.log("end outer loop");
}
//output:
//1,2,3,4,5,
//2,4,6,8,10,
```

for...of statement:

The for...of statement uses to Iterate over iterable objects (Array, arguments, Map, Set and so on).

Syntax:

```javascript
for (variable of object) {
    //statements
}
```

Example:

```javascript
const arr = [1, 2, 3, 4];
for (let val of arr) {
    console.log(val);
}

//output:
//1
//2
//3
```

for...in statement:

The for...in statement uses to iterate over all the enumerable properties of an object.

Syntax:

```
for (variable in object) {
    //statements
}
```

Example:

```
const car = {
    type: "fiat",
    model: 500,
    price: 5000
};
for (let prop in car) {
    console.log(prop + " : " + car[prop]);
}
//output:
//type : fiat
//model : 500
//price : 5000
```

In case of array for...in iterates over array indexes.

```
const arr = ["a", "b", "c"];
for (let index in arr) {
    console.log(index + " : " + arr[index]);
}
//output:
//0 : a
//1 : b
//2 : c
```

JavaScript Functions:

Functions are a set of statement (code line) or a code block which are written to achieve something. Function should take zero of more input and return an output where there is some obvious relationship between the input taken by function and the output return from the function. To use a function, you must define it somewhere in the scope from which you wish to call it.

Defining A function:

A JavaScript function is defined with the function keyword, followed by

1. The name of function
2. And the list of function's parameters (it may be zero or more), enclosed in parentheses ()
   and separated by commas (,).
3. The set of statement that defines JavaScript function, enclosed by curly brackets.

Syntax:

```
function function_name(param_1, param_2, ...param_N) {
    // A set of statements
}
```

Example:

```
function sum(num1, num2) {
return num1 + num2;
}
```

Calling a function:

Defining a function does not execute it.

Defining a function gives idea about what the function does when the function called.

Calling the function actually execute a set of statements or performs the specified actions with the indicated parameters.

For example, if you define the function sum, you can call it as follows:

Sum(10, 15)

The preceding statement calls the function with two arguments (10 and 15). The function executes its statements and returns the value 25.

See full example:

```
function sum(num1, num2) {
    return num1 + num2;
}
let result = sum(10, 15);
console.log(result); // 25
```

Many times, you would see function calling appear before it's declaration. But in actual JavaScript interpreter hoists all the function declaration at top.

We will know more about JavaScript hoisting later.

```
let result = sum(10, 15);
console.log(result); // 25

function sum(num1, num2) {
    return num1 + num2;
}
```

Anonymous Function:

In JavaScript, an anonymous function is a function that is declared without any name or identification. we cannot access or call an anonymous function after its declaration.
It can only be done by function literal.

Syntax:

```
function([parametes]) {
    //function body
}
```

Example:

```
let func = function () {
    console.log("Hi ! I am a anonymous function");
};
func();
//output:
//Hi ! I am a anonymous function
```

Function literals:

JavaScript 1.2 introduces the concept of **function literals** which is nothing special just a way of referring a function definition.

A function literal is an expression where we can assign an anonymous function definition to a variable, so that we can call it whenever needed.

Syntax:

```
Var/let/const variable_name = function (param_1, param_2, ...Param_N) {
//statements
}
```

Example:

```
const sum = function (num1, num2) {
    return num1 + num2;
}
let result = sum(10, 15);
console.log(result); // 25
```

Note: Function literals does not allow hoisting means if you are calling a method before it's declaration then it will give you an error.

```
let result = sum(10, 15);
console.log(result);

const sum = function (num1, num2) {
    return num1 + num2;
}

//output: ReferenceError: Cannot access 'sum' before initialization
```

Inner Function:

A function defined with in another function is call inner function.

The inner function can be accessed only from statements in the outer function.

Inner function can access the variables and arguments of outer function but outer function cannot access or use the variables and arguments of inner function. These forms of inner function declaration are called Closure. We will explain closure in more details later.

```
function outer() {
    console.log("outer function.");
    function inner() {
        console.log("inner function.");
    }
    inner();
}
outer();
//output:
//outer function.
//inner function.
```

Function Scope

Variables defined with in a function cannot be accessed from outside the function, because the scope of variable is limited to function in which it is defined. However, A function defined inside another function can also access all variables defined in its parent function, and any other variables which its parent can access.

```
//below variables are global
const num1 = 10, num2 = 15, num3 = 25;

//below function is defined in global scope
function sum() {
    return num1 + num2; //10(global) + 15(global)
}

//a nested function
function addNum() {
    const num1 = 2, num2 = 3;
    function add() {
        return num1 + num2 + num3; //10(local) + 15(local) +25(global)
    }
    return add();
}

const res1 = sum();
const res2 = addNum();
console.log(res1); //25
console.log(res2); //30
```

Note:

1. We can pass any number of arguments in a function and can get all the arguments with the help of **arguments** array.

    ```
    function sum() {
        return arguments[0] + arguments[1] + arguments[2];
    }

    const res1 = sum(2, 3, 5);
    console.log(res1); //10
    ```

2. We can pass any number of arguments out of n parameters in a function. These arguments always assigned from left to right and other parameter's value takes as 'Undefined'.

```
function print(num1, num2, num3, num4) {
    console.log(num1); //2
    console.log(num2); //3
    console.log(num3); //5
    console.log(num4); //undefined
}

print(2, 3, 5);
```

3. We can also initialize an argument with default value if no value passed from caller function, then the argument will use its default value.

```
function print(num1, num2, num3 = 3, num4 = 6) {
    console.log(num1); //2
    console.log(num2); //3
    console.log(num3); //5
    console.log(num4); //6 (default value because not argument passed for
num4)
}

print(2, 3, 5);
```

4. We can also use rest parameter to represent indefinite number of arguments as an array.In the below example, the function sum uses ***rest parameters*** to collect arguments from the third one to the end and return the sum of all parameters.

```
function sum(num1, num2, ...restArgs) {
    let sum = num1 + num2;
    restArgs.forEach(element => {
        sum += element;
    });
    return sum;
}

const res = sum(2, 3, 5, 4, 5, 6);
console.log(res); //25
```

Note: Rest parameter must be last formal parameter in the parameters list. And we can only use one parameter in parameter list.

Arrow function:

Arrow function is an alternative way to a traditional function. Or in simple words, this is a shorten syntax to declared a function.

There is no need to specify function keyword and function name.

We can declare an arrow function using paratheses () followed by an arrow (=>).

Arrow function doesn't have own this, arguments and super.

Syntax:

```
() => {
    //function body
}
```

Please note, curly brasses ({}) required only if there are multiple lines.

Example:

```
let func = () => {
    return "hello! I am an arrow function.";
}
console.log(func());
//output: hello! I am an arrow function.
```

Note: If you have only one line return statement with in arrow function then no need to use curly brasses ({}) and return keyword.

So above function can also be written as:

```
let func = () => "hello! I am an arrow function.";
console.log(func());
//output: hello! I am an arrow function.
```

Self Invoking Function:

As we know, there are various useful feature introduced in JavaScript, and the **Self-Invoking**

function is one of them.

Self-invoking function means a function that invokes as soon as it's defined.

To call a JavaScript function immediately, the definition of such function is written with in parentheses () set followed by another set of parentheses () after the function's definition.

Syntax:

```
(function [functionName]([parametes){
    //write code here
}) ([arguments]);
```

Note:

1. FunctionName, parameters and arguments are optional, it's depended on you to pass or not.

2. We can use a simple function, literal/anonymous function and an arrow function as self-invoked function. However, there is not meaning of simple function because we cannot call this after its self-call.

3. If needed, you can also call a self-invoked later, by assign its definition to a variable. Please see the below examples.

Example :

Using simple function:

```
let age = 10;
(function func(name) {
    console.log("Hi ! I am", name, "My age is", age);
})("Jonh");   //Hi ! I am Jonh My age is 10.
func("Jim"); //this will give you error.
```

Using function literal/Anomymous:

```javascript
let age = 10;
let func = null;
(func = function (name) {
    console.log("Hi ! I am", name, "My age is", age);
})("Jonh");
func("Jim");

//output:
//Hi ! I am Jonh My age is 10
//Hi ! I am Jim My age is 10
```

Using Arrow function:

```javascript
let age = 10;
let func = null;
(func = (name) => {
    console.log("Hi ! I am", name, "My age is", age);
})("Jonh");
func("Jim");
//output:
//Hi ! I am Jonh My age is 10
//Hi ! I am Jim My age is 10
```

Function Currying:

Function currying is only supported by functional programming language (JavaScript) and it's an advance technique. It allows to transform a function call with multiple arguments to multiple function with one argument.

How is it possible: 'to transform a function call with multiple arguments to multiple function with one argument'

This is possible to by returning an inner function from an outer function it may be N level and each function only takes one argument.

Let's see in the action:

Support we want to add two numbers using a function then we can write a simple function as below:

```
function sum(a, b) {
    return a + b;
}

let result = sum(10, 30);
console.log("Sum of above numbers =", result);
//output:
//Sum of above numbers = 40
```

Now transformation of the above function can be done as below to achieve the function currying:

```
function func(a) {
    return function (b) {
        return a + b;
    }
}
let sum = func(10);
let result = sum(20);
console.log("Sum of above numbers =", result);
  //output:
  //Sum of above numbers = 40
```

let's think a little complex scenario, support we want to write a sum function which can add any number of values. In that case we can use function currying as below:

```
function sum(a) {
    return function (b) {
        return b ? sum(a + b) : a;
    }
}
//output:
//Sum of above numbers = 150
```

Above function can also be written as below using arrow function and function literal:

```
let sum = (a) => (b) => b ? sum(a+b) : a ;
let result = sum(10)(20)(30)(40)(50)();
console.log("Sum of above numbers =",result);
//output:
//Sum of above numbers = 150
```

Callback function:

A function passes to another function as an argument is called callback function, which is then called from the outer function to complete some specific tasks.

In other words, a function received another function as an argument, then the received function is called callback function.

Syntax:

```
function functionName(callbackFuntion, par1, par2,…, parN) {
    //some code
    callbackFunction(arg1, arg2,…, argN);
}
```

Example:

```
function printName(name) {
    return `Mr ${name}`;
}
function greetings(callback, welcomeLine, name) {
    console.log(welcomeLine);
    let _name = callback(name);
    console.log(_name);
    console.log("***********");
}

greetings(printName, "You'r welcome", "Sonu");
greetings(printName, "Good morning", "Singh");

//output:
//You'r welcome
//Mr Sonu
//***********
//Good morning
//Mr Singh
//***********
```

In above example, a function (printName) passed to another function (greetings) as a argument. Hence 'printName' would be a callback function for function 'greetings'.

Closure in JavaScript:

A closure is an important JavaScript feature and allows us to access outer function scope with in inner function.

In simple words, an inner function can access scope of its parent function means an inner function can also access all variables defined in its parent function, and any other variables which its parent can access.

A closure is created when an inner function keeps the environment of the outer scope even after the outer function has been already executed

Example: Inner function

```javascript
function outer() {
    var title = "JavaScript"; // local variable created by outer
    function inner() {
        // inner() is the inner/child function, that forms the closure
        console.log(title); // access the variable declared in outer function
    }
    return inner();
}
outer();
//Output : JavaScript
```

In above example, inner() function is an inner/child function defined inside outer function and is only accessible with in outer function. The outer() function is also created a local variable named "tittle" but there is no local variable created with in inner() function. However, as per closure definition, the inner() function can access the local variable of outer() function and able to log the value "JavaScript".

Now below is the transformation of the above example to understand the closure in better way.

```
function outer() {
    var title = "JavaScript"; // local variable created by outer
    function inner() {
        // inner() is the inner/child function, that forms the closure
        console.log(title); // access the variable declared in outer function
    }
    return inner;
}
var inner = outer();
inner();
//Output : JavaScript
```

In above example, the code looks confusing and that the code still works. in simple term, the local variables of a function exist for just the duration till the function execution finishes. So outer() finishes executing, we might assume/expect that the title variable would not exist or not accessible. But the code still works as expected, Hence the functions in JavaScript form closures.

Timer Functions in JavaScript:

JavaScript timer functions are used to execute a specified function or a piece of code after a specified time gets over.

JavaScript provides below functions to execution a task after specified timer expires. These are timer functions.

- setTimeout function
- setInterval function

setTimeout function :

setTimeout function allows a set of code or a function to executes once after a given timer expires. You can use this function if you want to executes a function or set of code after a specified timer and only once.

Syntax:

```
setTimeout(funcRef, delay, par1, par2)
setTimeout(funcRef, delay, par1, par2, /* … ,*/ parN)
```

Please check the below description for more details:

funcRef: it's a function or function reference which executed after the given timer expires.

delay: it is a time in milliseconds, which means given function should wait equal number of milliseconds before execution and then executes automatically.

par1, par2,…,parN : these are optional arguments which may require to pass in function parametes if required.

Example:

```
setTimeout(function() {
    console.log("I executed from setTimeout ");
    console.timeEnd("after")
}, 100);
console.time("after")
console.log("Hello!")
//Output :
//Hello!
//I executed from setTimeout
//after: 101.456ms
```

Please note, In above example output, time may be little different but it gives you an idea about the timer after that the specified function in setTimeout executed.

We can also pass string in delay parameter but it should be convertible to number otherwise setTimeout function will take it as 0 (zero) delay.

Example 1:

```
setTimeout(function() {
    console.log("I executed from setTimeout ");
    console.timeEnd("after")
}, "100");  //it will automatically converted to number 100
console.time("after")
console.log("Hello!")
//Output :
//Hello!
//I executed from setTimeout
//after: 101.456ms (it may be little different)
```

Example 2:

```
setTimeout(function () {
    console.log("I executed from setTimeout ");
    console.timeEnd("after")
}, "100 hello"); //takes as 0 delay
console.time("after")
console.log("Hello!")
//output:
//Hello!
//I executed from setTimeout
//after: 5.276ms (may be little different)
```

The setTimeout() returns timeoutID as a number value. We can use this value in clearTimeout() as parameter to cancel the execution of a given timer function.

Example:

```
let timeoutId = setTimeout(function () {
    console.log("I executed from setTimeout ");
}, "100 hello");
clearTimeout(timeoutId);
console.log("Hello!")
//output : Hello!
```

setInterval function :

setInterval function allows a set of code or a function to executes repeatedly with a fixed time delay between each call.

You can use this function if you want to executes a function or set of code repeatedly (again and again) with a specified time delay between each call.

Syntax:

```
setInterval(funcRef, delay, par1, par2)
setInterval(funcRef, delay, par1, par2, /* … ,*/ parN)
```

Please check the below description for more details:

funcRef: it's a function or function reference which executed repeatedly with a fixed time delay between each call.

delay: it is a time in milliseconds, which means given function should wait equal number of milliseconds between two continuous calls (executions).

par1, par2,...,parN : these are optional arguments which may require to pass in function parameters if required.

Example:

```
let intervalId = setInterval(function () {
    console.log("I executed from setInterval ");
    console.timeEnd('after')
    console.time('after');
}, 100);
setTimeout(() => {
    clearInterval(intervalId)
}, 500)
console.time('after');
console.log("Hello!")

//Output :
//Hello!
//I executed from setInterval
//after: 100.189ms
//I executed from setInterval
//after: 102.609ms
//I executed from setInterval
//after: 103.857ms
//I executed from setInterval
//after: 103.725ms
```

Please note, In above example output, time may be little different but it gives you an idea about the time delay between each function call specified in setInterval() function.

The setInterval() returns intervalID as a number value. We can use this value in clearInterval() as parameter to cancel the execution of a given timer function.

In above example, we are calling clearInterval() function with in setTimeout().

Exception Handling in JavaScript:

An **'exception'** is something happened unexpected/abnormal with in program which requires special attention to handle.

In other words, an exception breaks the normal execution of the program and generated by some anomalous code.

To handle these exceptions in our program or code we need **exception handling.**

For example, a non-zero value divided by zero will result into infinity, means exception. Thus, with the help of exception handling, we can handle these conditions and safe our program to abnormal termination.

Type of Errors:

1. **Syntax Error:** A mistake done by the programmer in the pre-defined syntax/rule of a programming language

2. **Runtime Error:** An error occurs during the program execution after successful compilation of program. (**Example**: Divide by Zero)

3. **Logical Error:** Logical error is something that program doesn't produce desired output. This type of error will not terminate the program. In other word, errors with in programmer's algorithm is called Logical error. For fixing these types of error, programmer need to check his algorithm/program again and again. It's little difficult to find out but yes, this is only way to fix logical errors.

Error Object in JavaScript:

In JavaScript when a runtime error occurs, it creates an error object and throws.

Error object has some important properties as below:

1. **name:** Error name.
2. **message:** A small description about the error.

Below are some built in error objects:

EvalError:

It indicates that an **error related eval()** method. However, JavaScript never produces this error.

Example:

```
try {
    throw new EvalError("EvalError Description");
} catch (e) {
    console.log(e instanceof EvalError); // true
    console.log(e.message); // "EvalError Description"
    console.log(e.name); // "EvalError"
}
```

ReferenceError:

It occurs when a variable, programmer is using within the program or code is not present or accessible.

Example:

```
console.log(test); //ReferenceError: test is not defined

//Programmer can create ReferenceError as below:
try {
    throw new ReferenceError("ReferenceError Description");
} catch (e) {
    console.log(e instanceof ReferenceError); // true
    console.log(e.message); // "ReferenceError Description"
    console.log(e.name); // "ReferenceError"
}
```

RangeError:

It indicates that a user is not using value with in the allowed range. A RangeError can be created as below:

Example:

```
let age = 300;
try {
    if (age < 0 || age > 100) {
        throw new RangeError("The age must be between 0 and 100.");
    }
}
catch (exe) {
    console.log(exe instanceof RangeError); //true
    console.log(exe.message); //The age must be between 0 and 100.
}
```

InternalError:

It indicates that an error occurs within JavaScript engine.

TypeError:

It indicates that the operation is performing on an invalid type.

Example:

```
let str = "Hello";
try {
    str.calc();
}
catch (exe) {
    console.log(exe); //TypeError: str.calc is not a function
}

//A TypeError can be created as below:
try {
    throw new TypeError("TypeError Description");
} catch (e) {
    console.log(e instanceof TypeError); // true
    console.log(e.message); // "TypeError Description"
    console.log(e.name); // "TypeError"
}
```

SyntaxError:

It indicates that programmer has done some mistakes with pre-defined programming language syntax:

Example:

```javascript
let result = 10++10; // SyntaxError: Invalid left-hand side expression in
postfix operation

//A SyntaxError can be created as below:
try {
    throw new SyntaxError("SyntaxError Description");
} catch (e) {
    console.log(e instanceof SyntaxError); // true
    console.log(e.message); // "SyntaxError Description"
    console.log(e.name); // "SyntaxError"
}
```

URIError:

It indicates that a URI function is not used correctly.

Example:

```javascript
decodeURIComponent("%"); // URIError: URI malformed

//A URIError can be crated as below:
try {
    throw new URIError("URIError Description");
} catch (e) {
    console.log(e instanceof URIError); // true
    console.log(e.message); // "URIError Description"
    console.log(e.name); // "URIError"
}
```

Exception Handling Statements:

Below are the exception handling statements that can be used to handle the exceptions and safe the program from the unexpected termination.

1. throw
2. try...catch
3. try...catch...finally

1. **throw statement:**

   The 'throw' statement is used to **throw** the exception with specified value of the error.

Example:

```
let num = 9;
if (num % 2 === 0) {
    console.log("Number is even.")
}
else {
    throw "Please enter even number.";
}
```

Note: you can throw any type of value using the throw statement.

```
throw "String value"; // String type
throw 34; // Number type
throw false; // Boolean type
```

2. **try...catch statement:**

   try...catch statement is used to handle the exception which can be thrown by the throw statement or by the JavaScript engine.

   Syntax:

```
try {
    //statements may produce the exception
}
catch (exception) {
    //statements to handle the exception
}
```

   Please note, as per JavaScript standard, try block contains the code which may produce the exception and catch block contains the code to handle the exception thrown by the try block.

   Example: (Exception throw by programmer)

142

```javascript
let num = 10;
try {
    if (num / 2 > 5) {
        console.log("Number is greater than 10.");
    }
    else {
        throw "Please enter a number greater than 10.";
    }
}
catch (exe) {
    console.log("Exception thrown :", exe);
}

//output:
//Exception thrown : Please enter a number greater than 10.
```

Example: (Exception thrown by JavaScript)

```javascript
try {
    let res = 10++10;
}
catch (exe) {
    console.log(exe);
}

    //output:
    //SyntaxError: Invalid left-hand side expression in postfix operation
```

3. **try...catch...finally statement:**

Please note, the try...catch...finally statement is similar to try...catch statement followed by the finally block.

The finally block of the try...catch...finally statement is executed always either an exception is occurred or not.

Syntax:

```
try {
    //statements may produce the exception
}
catch (exception) {
    //statements to handle the exception
}
finally {
    //statements execute always
}
```

Note: The finally block is option, it depends on programmer to use this or not.

Example:

```
let num = 9;
try {
    if (num / 2 > 5) {
        console.log("Number is greater than 10.");
    }
    else {
        throw "Please enter a number greater than 10.";
    }
}
catch (exe) {
    console.log("Exception thrown :", exe);
}
finally {
    console.log("Always execution block.")
}

//output:
//Exception thrown : Please enter a number greater than 10.
//Always execution block.
```

Asynchronous JavaScript:

Asynchronous JavaScript or asynchronous programming is a way that allows your program to do multiple tasks at same time or to start a task and still be able to responsive for other events instead having wait for the task completion. Once the task has been finished, your program will display the result.

This is very use full for calling backend APIs or tasks which takes a noticeable amount of time.

As part of asynchronous programming, we will cover below topics:

1. Promise
2. Promises chaining
3. Fetch API/Consume APIs
4. Async/await

Promise:

The 'Promise' object is used to represent the eventually completed state an asynchronous task/operation and its returning value, either its success or failure.

A promise is always in one of below three states:

1. **pending**: this is the initial state of promise, means no result produced till now (neither fulfilled nor rejected).
2. **fulfilled**: This is the state when the operation has completed successfully.
3. **rejected**: This is the state when the operation has failed.

A promise, either fulfilled or rejected is called settled.

Syntax:

```
let promise = new Promise(function (resolve, reject) {
    // code takes some time to finish

    resolve(); // successful
    reject();  // error
});

// function within then wait for a settled/fulfilled promise
promise.then(
    function (value) { /* code if successful */ },
    function (error) { /* code if some error */ }
)
    .catch(function (exception) {/* code if exception */ })
    .finally(function (info) {/* code runs after a promise either fulfilled or
rejected);
```

No worries, for better understanding we will see a couple of examples for each function (then, catch, finally).

Example:

```
function success(msg) {
    console.log("Success :", msg);
}
function failure(msg) {
    console.log("Failure :", msg);
}
let promise = function () {
    return new Promise(function (resolve, reject) {
        setTimeout(function () {
            if (Math.random() > .5)
                resolve("Numer is greater than .5.");
            else
                reject("Number is less than .5.");
        }, 1000);
    });
}
let myPromise = promise(); //this line return a promise
myPromise
    .then(success, failure);
//output:
//Success : Numer is greater than .5. (when fulfilled) OR
//Failure : Number is less than .5. (when failed)
```

Above example either print Success : Numer is greater than .5. (when fulfilled) or Failure : Number is less than .5. (when failed).

When a number is greater than .5 then we call resolve with returning result, means a promise has fulfilled else we call reject with returning result, means a promise has rejected/failed and the respective callback method of **'then'** is called based on the promise (fulfilled or failed).

then method:

The 'then()' method is used to attach a fulfillment and rejection handlers to the promise.

In other words, the 'then()' method of a promise takes up to two callback functions, one for the fulfilled case of the promise and other for the rejected case of the promise. A callback function uses for rejection case is optional, and we can also use 'catch()' method of promise object instead.

You can see the above example for the 'then()' method.

catch method :

As discussed, we can use the 'catch()' method of promise object instead of a callback function passed in 'then()' method for the rejected case of the promise.

The 'catch()' method of promise object takes a callback function as argument for the rejected case of promise.

Please see below example, this works same as previous example.

```
function success(msg) {
    console.log("Success :", msg);
}

function failure(msg) {
    console.log("Failure :", msg);
}

let promise = function () {
    return new Promise(function (resolve, reject) {
        setTimeout(function () {
            if (Math.random() > .5)
                resolve("Numer is greater than .5.");
            else
                reject("Number is less than .5.");
        }, 1000);
    });
}

let myPromise = promise(); //this line return a promise
myPromise
    .then(success)
    .catch(failure)

//output:
//Success : Numer is greater than .5. (when fulfilled)
//Failure : Number is less than .5. (when failed)
```

In above example, when a number is greater than .5 then we call resolve with returning result, means a promise has fulfilled and then the callback function of 'then()' is called.

When a number is less than .5 the we call reject with returning result, means a promise has rejected/failed and then the callback function of 'catch()' is called.

finally method:

The 'finally()' method of promise object takes a callback function as argument which calls immediately after a promise settled (either fulfilled or failed).

Example:

```
function success(msg) {
    console.log("Success :", msg);
}

function failure(msg) {
    console.log("Failure :", msg);
}

function final() {
    console.log("End of program!")
}

let promise = function () {
    return new Promise(function (resolve, reject) {
        setTimeout(function () {
            if (Math.random() > .5)
                resolve("Numer is greater than .5.");
            else
                reject("Number is less than .5.");
        }, 1000);
    });
}

let myPromise = promise(); //this line return a promise
myPromise
    .then(success)
    .catch(failure)
    .finally(final)

//output:
//Success : Numer is greater than .5. (when fulfilled)
//End of program!
//(OR)
//Failure : Number is less than .5. (when failed)
//End of program!
```

Note: the 'finally()' method of promise object is very usefull when you want to execute some code or action in any case either a promise is fulfilled or failed.

Above example code can also be written using arrow function, to make it clear and shorter. Please check below code which will produce the same result as above example.

```
let promise = () => {
    return new Promise((resolve, reject) => {
        setTimeout(() => {
            Math.random() > .5 ?
                resolve("Numer is greater than .5.")
                :
                reject("Number is less than .5.")
        }, 1000);
    });
}

promise()
    .then((msg) => console.log("Success :", msg))
    .catch((msg) => console.log("Failure :", msg))
    .finally(() => console.log("End of program!"))

//output:
//Success : Numer is greater than .5. (when fulfilled)
//End of program!
//(OR)
//Failure : Number is less than .5. (when failed)
//End of program!
```

Promise chaining:

Promise chaining is a way to fulfilled multiple promises one after another.

It is very useful when you want to perform multiple asynchronous operation and one operation is dependent to another.

The methods 'then()', 'catch()' and 'finally()' of promise object are used to attached further action with a promise, either its fulfilled or rejected. You can be chained return result of these methods, as these methods return promises.

Example:

```javascript
let promise = new Promise((resolve, reject) => {
    setTimeout(() => {
        let number = Math.random();
        number > .5 ?
            resolve(number * 10)
            :
            reject(number * 5)
    }, 1000);
});


promise
    .then((res) => {
        console.log("fulfilled1", res);
        return res * 10;
    }, (err) => {
        console.log("rejected1", err);
        return err * 5;
    })
    .then((res) => {
        console.log("fulfilled2", res);
        return res * 10;
    }, (err) => {
        console.log("rejected2", err);
        return err * 5;
    })
    .finally(() => console.log("End of program!"))

//output:
//fulfilled1 [numer]
//fulfilled2 [numer]
//End of program
//(OR)
//rejected1 [numer]
//fulfilled2 [numer]
//End of program
```

Please note, above example never prints 'rejected2'. Because any value returns from any 'then()' action handler, works as fulfilled promise for next 'then()' method. Hence, fulfilled action executes.

However, you can also return a promise from any 'then()' action handler. Which will work expected either fulfilled promise or rejected promise for next 'then()' method.

Example:

```
let promise = new Promise((resolve, reject) => {
    setTimeout(() => {
        let number = Math.random();
        number > .5 ?
            resolve(number * 10)
            :
            reject(number * 5)
    }, 1000);
});
```

```
promise
    .then((res) => {
        console.log("fulfilled1", res);
        return Promise.resolve(res * 10);
    }, (err) => {
        console.log("rejected1", err);
        return Promise.reject(err * 5);
    })
    .then((res) => {
        console.log("fulfilled2", res);
    }, (err) => {
        console.log("rejected2", err);
    })
    .finally(() => console.log("End of program!"))
```

```
//output:
//fulfilled1 [numer]
//fulfilled2 [numer]
//End of program
//(OR)
//rejected1 [numer]
//rejected2 [numer]
//End of program
```

You can call or attach multiple 'then()' method with a promise.

```javascript
let promise = new Promise((resolve, reject) => {
    setTimeout(() => {
        resolve(5);
    }, 1000);
});

promise.then((result) => {
    console.log("First", result);
})

promise.then((result) => {
    console.log("Second", result);
})

promise.then((result) => {
    console.log("Third", result);
});

//output:
//First 5
//Second 5
//Third 5
```

Below are important methods of Promise class. These offers us to work with promise in better way.

resolve() method:

The 'resolve()' method of promise 'resolves' a value to a promise. If the resolve value is a promise, then the same promise is returned. If the value is thenable, 'resolve()' will call 'then()' method with both action handlers (fulfilled and rejected).

Example1: resoling a promise

```javascript
let promise = Promise.resolve("hello!");
promise.then((result) => {
    console.log(result);
});
//output: hello!
```

Example2: resolving thenables

```
let promise = Promise.resolve(
    {
        then(resolve, reject) {
            reject("promise rejected.");
        }
    });
promise.then((result) => {
    console.log(result); //not called
}, (error) => {
    console.log("Error:", error)
});
//output: Error: promise rejected.
```

reject() method:

The reject()' method of promise 'rejects' a value to a promise.

Example:

```
let promise = Promise.reject("promise rejected.");
promise.then((result) => {
    console.log(result); //not called
}, (error) => {
    console.log("Error:", error)
});
//output: Error: promise rejected.
```

all() method:

The 'all()' method of promise takes an array of promise as input and return a single promise.

If the all-input's promises return fulfills then 'all()' method returns a promise fulfill with an array of all fulfillment values.

If the any of input's promise return rejects, then 'all()' method returns a promise reject with first rejection reason.

Example1: when all input's promises return fulfills

```
let p1 = Promise.resolve("Promise 1 resolved.");
let p2 = "Promise 2 resolved.";
let p3 = new Promise((resolve, reject) => {
    setTimeout(() => resolve("Promise 3 resolved."), 1000);
})

Promise
    .all([p1, p2, p3])
    .then((result) => {
        console.log(result);
    }, (error) => {
        console.log("Error:", error) // not called
    });

//output:
//[ 'Promise 1 resolved.', 'Promise 2 resolved.', 'Promise 3 resolved.' ]
```

Example2: when some of input's promises return rejects.

```
let p1 = Promise.resolve("Promise 1 resolved.");
let p2 = new Promise((resolve, reject) => {
    setTimeout(() => reject("Promise 2 resolved."), 2000);
});
let p3 = new Promise((resolve, reject) => {
    setTimeout(() => reject("Promise 3 rejected."), 1000);
});

Promise
    .all([p1, p2, p3])
    .then((result) => {
        console.log(result); //not called
    }, (error) => {
        console.log("Error:", error)
    });

//output:
//Error: Promise 3 rejected.
```

any() method:

The 'any()' method of promise takes an array of promise as input and return a single promise.

If the one of input's promises return fulfill then 'any()' method returns a promise fulfill with first fulfilled promise.

Example:

```
let p1 = Promise.reject("Promise 1 reject.");
let p2 = "Promise 2 resolved.";
let p3 = new Promise((resolve, reject) => {
    setTimeout(() => resolve("Promise 3 resolved."), 1000);
});

Promise
    .any([p1, p2, p3])
    .then((result) => {
        console.log(result); //not called
    }, (error) => {
        console.log("Error:", error)
    });

//output:
//Promise 2 resolved.
```

race() method:

The race()' method of promise takes an array of promise as input and return a single promise.

If the one of input's promises return either fulfill or reject then 'race()' method returns either a promise fulfills with first fulfilled promise or reject with first rejection promise.

Example:

```
let p1 = Promise.reject("Promise 1 reject.");
let p2 = Promise.resolve("Promise 2 resolved.");
let p3 = new Promise((resolve, reject) => {
    setTimeout(() => resolve("Promise 3 resolved."), 1000);
});

Promise
    .race([p1, p2, p3])
    .then((result) => {
        console.log(result); //not called
    }, (error) => {
        console.log("Error:", error)
    });

//output:
//Error: Promise 1 reject.
```

allSettled() method:

The **allSettled()**' method of promise takes an array of promise as input and return a single promise. If the all-input's promises are settled (fulfilled or rejected) then 'allSettled()' method returns a promise fulfill with an array of all promise's values (fulfileed or rejected).

Example:

```javascript
let p1 = Promise.reject("Promise 1 reject.");
let p2 = Promise.resolve("Promise 2 resolved.");
let p3 = new Promise((resolve, reject) => {
    setTimeout(() => resolve("Promise 3 resolved."), 1000);
});

Promise
    .allSettled([p1, p2, p3])
    .then((result) => {
        console.log(result);
    }, (error) => {
        console.log("Error:", error); //not called
    });

//output:
//[
//  { status: 'rejected', reason: 'Promise 1 reject.' },
//  { status: 'fulfilled', value: 'Promise 2 resolved.' },
//  { status: 'fulfilled', value: 'Promise 3 resolved.' }
//]
```

Fetch API/Consume APIs:

The Fetch API provides a better way to call APIs in JavaScript using global fetch() method. It is a promised-based interface for fetching resources using HTTP requests to server from the browser.

The fetch method:

The 'fetch()' method provides a better, easy, logical way to fetch resources by making HTTP requests across the network.

Previously, we can achieve the same using XMLHttpRequest, but now fetch() method is a good alternative.

Using fetch() method, we can call either a GET request (for getting data) or POST request (for posting data).

Syntax:

```
fetch('serviceUrl',[options])
    .then(response => {
        //handle API response
    })
    .then(data => {
        //handle API data
    })
    .catch(error => {
        //handle API error
    })
    .finally(final => {
        //some code in finally if needed
    });
```

Example:

```
fetch('GET_API_URL')
    .then(respose => {
        return respose.json();
    })
    .then(data => {
        console.log(data)
    })
    .catch(error => {
        console.log(error)
    })
```

Please note, options parameter is optional in fetch() method in some cases (like above get request example), but in case of post and any other request it needed to specify.

options parameter is type of object which contains below properties:

1. **Method**: we can specify request method as string (GET, POST, PUT, DELETE)

2. **Headers**: use for API header setting or passing some data in header (like: content-type, authorization-tocken and more)

3. **Body**: use for passing the data in API, it can be following: Body.array.Buffer(), Body.Blob(), Body.formData(), Body.json(), Body.text().

4. **Mode** : no-cors, *cors, same-origin

5. **Credentials**: include, *same-origin, omit

6. **Cache**: *default, no-cache, reload, force-cache, only-if-cached

Syntax:

```
fetch("API_URL", {
    method: "POST", // GET, POST, PUT, DELETE, more
    mode: "cors", //same-origin, no-cors, cors
    cache: "no-cache", // default, no-cache, reload, force-cache, only-if-
cached
    credentials: "same-origin", // include, same-origin, omit
    headers: {
        "Content-Type": "application/json",
        //application/json, text/html, application/x-www-form-urlencoded',
many more
    },
    body: JSON.stringify(data), // body type must match with "Content-Type"
})
    .then(response => {
        return response.json()
    })
    .then(data => {
        console.log(date);
    })
    .catch(error => {
        console.log(error);
    })
```

Async/await:

The async/await is a comfortable and cleaner way to work with promise-based asynchronous program or code.

With the help of the async/await syntax we can ignore or minimize the uses of unnecessary chain of promises.

We can declare the async function using the **async** keyword where the **await** keyword can be used with the function body to call a promise-based function.

Syntax:

```
async function functionName(par1, par2,…, parN) {
    //code
    await calledFunction()
    //other code
}
```

Note:

1. Calling function: A function call another function with in this body is called a calling.

2. Called function: A function called from another function's body.

3. The await can only be used with in async function.

We will write a code using **promises** first and then convert the same using **async/await** for better understanding and noticing the difference.

Example (Promises):

```
function taskOneResolveAfter2Secs() {
    return new Promise((resolve, reject) => {
        setTimeout(function () {
            resolve("Task one resolved after 2 seconds.")
        }, 2000);
    });
}
function taskTwoResolveAfter1Secs() {
    return new Promise((resolve, reject) => {
        setTimeout(function () {
            resolve("Task two resolved after 1 second.")
        }, 1000);
    });
}
function printResult() {
    const p1 = taskOneResolveAfter2Secs();
    p1.then((res) => {
        console.log(res);
        const p2 = taskTwoResolveAfter1Secs();
        p2.then((res1) => {
            console.log(res1);
        })
    })
}
printResult();
//output:
//Task one resolved after 2 seconds.
//Task two resolved after 1 second.
```

Example (async/await): here we will replace above 'printResult()' method using async/await keywords.

```
async function printResult() {
    const p1 = await taskOneResolveAfter2Secs();
    console.log(p1);
    const p2 = await taskTwoResolveAfter1Secs();
    console.log(p2);
}
printResult();
//output:
//Task one resolved after 2 seconds.
//Task two resolved after 1 second.
```

In above examples you can see the differences in calling the promise-based function. In first example we are using multiple '**then()**' methods with in '**printResult**()' function but in second example there is no method. However, both examples produce the same result.

We can't use await with in another function if this is not declared with async keyword. If you use await anywhere other than async then you will get **SyntaxError**.

Handle Exceptions with async/await:

As we know, using promise chaining we can handle the exception using 'catch()' method but async/await provides us to handle errors with try/catch blocks as we did in simple JavaScript. Please check the below example:

```javascript
function taskOneResolveAfter2Secs() {
    return new Promise((resolve, reject) => {
        setTimeout(function () {
            reject("Task one rejected after 2 seconds.")
        }, 2000);
    });
}

function taskTwoResolveAfter1Secs() {
    return new Promise((resolve, reject) => {
        setTimeout(function () {
            resolve("Task two resolved after 1 second.")
        }, 1000);
    });
}
async function printResult() {
    try {
        const p1 = await taskOneResolveAfter2Secs();
    }
    catch (exe) {
        console.log("Exception:", exe);
    }
    const p2 = await taskTwoResolveAfter1Secs();
    console.log(p2);
}
printResult();
//output:
//Exception: Task one rejected after 2 seconds.
//Task two resolved after 1 second.
```

You can also replace the above 'printFunction()' with the below alternative where you can use 'catch()' method to chain the promise and produce the same result.

```javascript
async function printResult() {
    const p1 = await taskOneResolveAfter2Secs()
        .catch(exe => {
            console.log("Exception:", exe);
        });
    const p2 = await taskTwoResolveAfter1Secs();
    console.log(p2);
}
```

Fetch API with async/await:

As you already know about Fetch API, as discussed in previous section. In that section we are using 'then()' and 'catch()' methods of Promise to handle the response return from the fetch API.

The async/await can also be used for same purpose to write the more comfortable and cleaner code.

Let's see below example:

```javascript
function getResult() {
    fetch('API_URL')
        .then(respose => {
            return respose.json();
        })
        .then(data => {
            console.log(data)
        })
        .catch(error => {
            console.log(error)
        })
}
getResult();
```

In above example, we are handling the return result of API using 'then()' and 'catch()' method of Promise class. Now we will write the same code using async/await keywords.

```javascript
async function getResult() {
    try {
        const res = await fetch('API_URL');
        const data = await res.json();
        console.log(data)
    }
    catch (error) {
        console.log(error)
    }
}
getResult();
```

Please note, Above example is just a way to explain that how can we use fetch API with async/await.

For more information about Fetch API, please read the Fetch API section described in previous section.

JavaScript Browser BOM:

The Browser Object Model (BOM) is used to interact JavaScript actions with the browser.

1. The 'window' object
2. The 'history' object
3. The 'location' object
4. The 'navigator' object
5. The 'screen' object

The window Object:

The 'window' object referenced to the browser's window.

In other words, this is the default object of browser it represents the browser window.

The window object is a browser object not JavaScript.

All the global variables, object and function automatically associate with the window object.

1. Global variables become properties of window object

2. Global functions become methods of window object

```
> window._var
< 10
> _var
< 10
>
```

❌ No errors
⚠️ No warnings
ℹ️ No info
⚙️ No verbose

Please note, in above example **_var** is a global variable which can be access either using window object or directly.

So, **window.** is option its totally up to you either use this or not.

Note: Either use either browser console or a JavaScript file for all future example to get the desired result.

There are some important methods of window object:

alert(): This method is used to display a dialog with a message and 'OK' button on browser window.
Syntax:
```
window.alert(msg);
alert(msg);
```
Example:
```
window.alert(" Alert msg ");
```

confirm(): This method is used to display a dialog with a message and two buttons (OK an Cancel) on the browser window.

Syntax:
```
window.confirm(msg);
confirm(msg);
```
Example:
```
window.confirm(" Confirm msg ");
```

prompt(): This method is used to display a dialog with an input box to get an input from the user.
Syntax:
```
window.prompt(msg);
prompt(msg);
```
Example:
```
window.prompt("Enter value for age");
```

open(): Used to open a new window.

close(): Used to close the current window.

The 'setTimeout' and 'setInterval' methods are also window method. We are not going to explain these here because we have discussed this method already (See: Timer Function Section).

The history Object:

The **'history'** object is a global object. You can access this either using window object or without. The 'history' object contains an array of all visited URLs in your browser and very help full if you want to load your browser previous page, forward page and any particular visited page.

We can use length property of history object to know the length of the history URLs.

Important methods of history object:

forward(): This method is used to load the next forwarded page.
Syntax:
```
window.history.forward();
history.forward();
```

back(): This method is used to load the last visited page.
Syntax:
```
window.history.back();
history.back();
```

go(): This method is used to load the specified visited page.

Syntax:
```
history.go(num);
```

Note: when num is positive then it loads the forwarded visited page else loads the previous visited page.

The location Object:

The **'location'** object is also a global object. You can access this either using window object or without.

The 'location' object can be used to get information about the current page address (URL) and set the new page URL to redirect on a new page.

You can load new page using **'assign()'** method of location object. As,

window.location.assign("new page url");

Below are some important properties of location object:

href: This property is used to get the URL of the current page
Syntax:
```
window.location.href;
location.href;
```

hostname: This property is used to get domain name from the current page URL.
Syntax:
```
window.location.hostname;
location.hostname;
```

pathname: This property is used to get the **URL after hostname** from the current URL
Syntax:

```
window.location.pathname;
location.pathname;
```

protocol: This property is used to get the **protocol** used for accessing the current URL.
Syntax:

```
window.location.protocol;
location.protocol;
```

Please check below image for more information about (https://www.mozilla.org/en-US/firefox/)

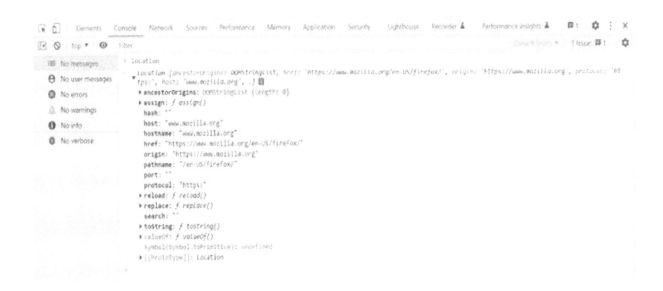

The navigator object:

The 'navigator' object can be used to get the information about visitor's browser.

The **'navigator'** object is also a global object. You can access this either using window object or without.

You can use **'javaEnabled()'** method of navigator object to know that java is enabled or not.

Below are some important properties of 'navigator' object:

appName: This property returns the browser's application name.
Syntax:
```
window.navigator.appName;
navigator.appName;
```


appVersion: This property returns the browser's application version.

Syntax:
```
window.navigator.appVersion;
navigator.appVersion;
```


cookieEnabled: This property returns true if browser cookie is enabled else returns false.

Syntax:
```
window.navigator.cookieEnabled;
navigator.cookieEnabled;
```


platform: This property returns the browser platform value.

Syntax:
```
window.navigator.platform;
navigator.platform;
```


online: This property returns true if browser is online else returns false.

Syntax:
```
window.navigator.online;
```

Please check below image for more information:

The screen object:

The 'screen' object can be used to get the information about browser's screen.

Like: screen width and height, pixelDepth and more.

The **'screen'** object is also a global object. You can access this either using window object or without.

Below are some important properties of 'screen' object:

width: This property returns width of the screen.

Syntax:
```
window.screen.width;
screen.width;
```

availWidth: This property returns available width of screen.

Syntax:

```
window.screen.availWidth;
screen.availWidth;
```

height: This property returns height of the screen.

Syntax:
```
window.screen.height;
screen.height;
```

availHeight: This property returns available height of screen.

Syntax:
```
window.screen.availHeight;
screen.availHeight;
```

colorDepth: This property returns color depth of the screen.

Syntax:
```
window.screen.colorDepth;
screen.colorDepth;
```

pixelDepth: This property returns pixel depth of the screen.

Syntax:
```
window.screen.pixelDepth;
screen.pixelDepth;
```

Please check below image for more information:

Document Object Model (DOM)

A browser creates Document Object Model when a web page is loaded in it and JavaScript can access any element of the document and update their content, structure and style.

According to W3C - "The W3C Document Object Model (DOM) is a platform and language-neutral interface that allows programs and scripts to dynamically access and update the content, structure, and style of a document."

The Document Object Model (DOM) is created as tree structure:

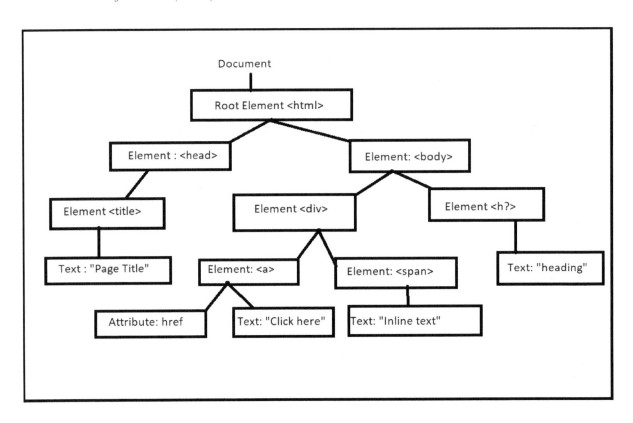

JavaScript has all the power to perform the below action by accessing the document/element.

- JavaScript can change/update all the HTML elements, their attributes and styles

- JavaScript can append/insert new HTML elements and attributes

- JavaScript can delete existing HTML elements and attributes

Please note, in this (DOM) section we will not going to explain everything related to HTML & JavaScript. However, we will try to cover most of important things.

1. Accessing/retrieving element(s) from the document

2. Add/insert an element into document

3. Remove an element from the document

4. Updating content of an element

5. Updating attribute value of an element

6. Adding/updating style of an element

7. JavaScript Events

1. Accessing/retrieving element(s) from the document

To retrieving or accessing element(s) from the document, document object has some important methods.

getElementById(*id*)
It returns the element based on the element-id if no element found then returns null.

Syntax:
```
document.getElementById(id)
```

Example:
If you want to get an element by **id="main_div"**, then you can use below:
```
document.getElementById("main_div")
```

getElementsByTagName(*name*)
It returns all the elements based on the tag name.

Syntax:
```
document.getElementsByTagName(tag_name)
```

Example:

If you want to get all the <p> elements from the document, then you can use below:
```
document.getElementsByTagName("p")
```

getElementsByClassName(*name*)

It returns all the elements based on the class name.

Syntax:
```
document.getElementsByClassName(class_name)
```

Example:

If you want to get all the elements based on their class (class="outer"), then you can use below:
```
document.getElementsByClassName("outer")
```

querySelector(query)

It returns first element based on the query.

Syntax:
```
document.querySelector(query)
```

Example:

If you want to get first element based on their class (class="outer"), then you can use below:
```
document.querySelector(".outer")
//Get by id (id = "header")
document.querySelector("#header")
//Get by tag name (<p>)
document.querySelector("p")
//Get first <p> element where class = "outer"
document.querySelector("p.outer")
```

querySelectorAll(query)

It returns all the elements based on the query.

Syntax:
```
document.querySelectorAll(query)
```

Example:

If you want to get all the elements based on their class (class="outer"), then you can use below:

```
document.querySelectorAll(".outer")
//Get all <p> elements by tag name
document.querySelectorAll("p")
//Get all <p> elements where class = "outer"
document.querySelectorAll("p.outer")
```

If the above example is not clear now, don't worry you will see a combined example in upcoming sections.

2. Add/insert an element into document:

You can add/insert an element into document using below methods:

append(*element/string*)

Using append method, you can append Node objects or string objects after the last child element.

Syntax:

```
element.append(element|string)
```

Example:

If you want to add a div element into another div with id = "outer" then you can use below:

```
let outerEle = document.getElementById("outer");
let innerDiv = document.createElement("div"); //create new div
outerEle.append(innerDiv); //append new div into outer div
```

appendChild(*element*)

this is similar to append but accept only Node object not string object

Syntax:

```
element.appendChild(element)
```

Example:

If you want to add a div element into another div with id = "outer" then you can use below:

```
let outerEle = document.getElementById("outer");
let innerDiv = document.createElement("div"); //create new div
outerEle.appendChild(innerDiv); //append new div into outer div
```

You can also use **innerHTML** property for the same purpose as below:

Above example can also be written as:

```
let outerEle = document.getElementById("outer");
let innerDiv = '<div> Inner Div </div>'; //create div as string
outerEle.innerHTML += innerDiv; //append new div into outer div
```

3. Remove an element from the document:

You can use document.removeChild(element) method to remove an element from the document.

Example: If you want to remove an element with id = "outer" from the document then you can use below:

```
let outerEle = document.getElementById("outer"); //get element with id =
"outer"
Let innerEle = document.getElementById("inner"); //get element with id =
"inner"
outerEle.removeChild(innerEle); // remove inner element from outer element
```

Let's see an example now:

main.html

```html
<!doctype html>
<html lang="en">

<head>
    <meta charset="utf-8">
    <title>test program</title>
    <script src="./main.js" type="text/JavaScript"></script>
</head>

<body>

    <h2>JavaScript HTML DOM Example</h2>
    <button id="btn1">Get element by
getElementsByClassName("outerDiv")</button><br /><br />
    <button id="btn2">Get element by querySelector("#btn2")</button><br /><br
/>
    <button id="btn3">Append a new div in div (id="div3")</button><br /><br />
    <button id="btn4">Remove divs from div (id = "div3")</button><br /><br />
    <div id="div1" class="outerDiv">
        Div (id="div1" class="outerDiv")
    </div>
    <br />
    <div id="div2">
        Div (id="div2")
    </div>
    <br />
    <div id="div3" class="outerDiv">
        Div (id="div3" class="outerDiv")
    </div>
    <br />
    <div id="div4">
        Div (id="div4")
    </div>
    <br />
    <div id="div5" class="outerDiv">
        Div (id="div5" class="outerDiv")
    </div>
    <br />
    <div id="resultDiv"></div>
```

```
<style>
        div {
            background-color: red;
            color: white;
        }

        .outerDiv {
            background-color: blue;
        }

        #resultDiv {
            border: solid 5px green;
            min-height: 100px;
        }
    </style>
</body>

</html>
```

Main.js

```
document.addEventListener("DOMContentLoaded", () => {
    //get all button using getElementById
    let btn1 = document.getElementById("btn1");
    let btn2 = document.getElementById("btn2");
    let btn3 = document.getElementById("btn3");
    let btn4 = document.getElementById("btn4");

    //add event listener to all div using addEventListener() method
    btn1.addEventListener("click", divOneClickFunc);
    btn2.addEventListener("click", divTwoClickFunc);
    btn3.addEventListener("click", divThreeClickFunc);
    btn4.addEventListener("click", divFourClickFunc);
```

```javascript
//function's declaration
    function divOneClickFunc() {
        //get elements by class name
        let elements = document.getElementsByClassName("outerDiv");
        //get element by id
        let resultDiv = document.getElementById("resultDiv");
        resultDiv.innerHTML = '';
        for (let index = 0; index < elements.length; index++) {
            //display content of all divs in result div using innerHTML
property
            resultDiv.innerHTML += elements[index].textContent + "<br>";
        }
    }

    function divTwoClickFunc() {
        //get element by querySelector
        let element = document.querySelector("#btn2");
        let resultDiv = document.getElementById("resultDiv");
        //display content in result div
        resultDiv.innerHTML = element.textContent;
    }

    let id = 0;
    function divThreeClickFunc() {
        let element = document.createElement("div");
        element.id = "new" + id;
        id++;
        element.textContent = "This is new div";
        let div3 = document.getElementById("div3");
        //append an element into a div (id = div3)
        div3.append(element);
    }

    function divFourClickFunc() {
        id--;
        let newDiv = document.getElementById("new" + id);
        let div3 = document.getElementById("div3");
        //remove an element from div3
        div3.removeChild(newDiv);
    }
});
```

4. Updating content of an element:

You can use below JavaScript properties to set/get content into/from an element.

A. innerText

```
element.innerText = "content you want to set";
```

B. textContent

```
element.textContent = "content you want to set";
```

Both properties are similar to each other except below differences:

1. **textContent** returns text content of all elements, but **innerText** returns the text content all elements except <script> and <style>.
2. **textContent** can be used to get the content of hidden element, but **innerText** cannot be used.

5. Updating attribute value of an element:

For updating attribute value of an element, you can use one of the below:

A. setAttribute(attribute, value) method

```
element.setAttribute("name", "elementName")
```

B. attribute property

```
element.name = "elementName";
```

If the above example is not clear now, don't worry you will see a combined example in upcoming sections.

6. Adding/updating style of an element:

For updating style property value of an element, you can use one of the below:

A. style.setProperty(propertyName, value) method

```
element.style.setProperty("color", "red")
```

B. Style.[propertyName]

```
element.style.color = "red";
```

Please see a below example for better understanding of above topics.

Main.html

```html
<!doctype html>
<html lang="en">

<head>
    <meta charset="utf-8">
    <title>test program</title>
    <script src="./main.js" type="text/JavaScript"></script>
</head>

<body>

    <h2>JavaScript HTML DOM Example</h2>
    <button id="btn1">Change div-1 content</button><br /><br />
    <button id="btn2">Change button-3 name</button><br /><br />
    <button id="btn3">Button-3</button><br /><br />
    <button id="btn4">Change back ground color of divs</button><br /><br />
    <div id="div1" class="outerDiv">
        div-1
    </div>
```

```html
    <br />
    <div id="div2">
        div-2
    </div>
    <style>
        div {
            background-color: red;
            border: solid 5px green;
            min-height: 100px;
        }
    </style>
</body>

</html>
```

Main.js:

```javascript
document.addEventListener("DOMContentLoaded", () => {
    //get all button using getElementById
    let btn1 = document.getElementById("btn1");
    let btn2 = document.getElementById("btn2");
    let btn4 = document.getElementById("btn4");

    //add event listener to all div using addEventListener() method
    btn1.addEventListener("click", divOneClickFunc);
    btn2.addEventListener("click", divTwoClickFunc);
    btn4.addEventListener("click", divFourClickFunc);

    //function's declaration
    function divOneClickFunc() {
        //get div 1
        let element = document.getElementById("div1");
        //udpate content
        element.textContent = "This is div-1";
    }
```

```javascript
    function divTwoClickFunc() {
        //get element by querySelector
        let element = document.querySelector("#btn3");
        //set button name
        element.name = "button-3";
        //get button by udpated name
        element = document.getElementsByName("button-3")[0];
        //change content of button
        element.textContent = "This is button-3";
    }

    function divFourClickFunc() {

        let div1 = document.getElementById("div1");
        let div2 = document.getElementById("div2");
        //change background color and color of divs
        div1.style.backgroundColor = "blue";
        div1.style.color = "white";
        div2.style["background-color"] = "blue";
        div2.style.setProperty("color", "white");
    }
});
```

7. JavaScript Events:

The Events are things that happen over HTML element. In JavaScript, there are many events which represent that some action is performed on a HTML element by the user/browser.

When an event occurs then some code runs automatically to handle the produced action/event.

JavaScript has many types of events to perform the deferent tasks:

Example:

1. The user presses a key on the keyboard

2. The user clicks or hovers the mouse over an HTML element

3. The user resizes the browser window

4. The web page fully loaded

5. Change content in input elements

6. And more

Below are some important events:

Mouse Events:

Event	Description
onclick	Occurs when the user clicks on an HTML element
oncontextmenu	Occurs when the user clicks right button of mouse on an HTML element
ondblclick	Occurs when the user double clicks on an HTML element
onmouseenter	Occurs when the cursor of mouse enters onto an HTML element.
onmouseleave	Occurs when the cursor of mouse leaves an HTML element.
onmousemove	Occurs when the cursor of mouse moves over an HTML element
onmouseout	Occurs when the cursor of mouse moved out from an HTML element
onmouseover	Occurs when the cursor of mouse moved over an HTML element
onmousedown	Occurs when the user pressed the mouse button over an HTML element.
onmouseup	Occurs when the user released the mouse button over an HTML element.

Keyboard events:

Event	Description
onkeydown	Occurs when the user presses a key from keyboard
onkeypress	Occurs when the user pressed a key from keyboard
onkeyup	Occurs when the user released a key from keyboard

Form events:

Event	Description
onfocus	Occurs when the user focuses a form element

onblur	Occurs when the user focuses out from a form element
onsubmit	Occurs when the user submits the form
onchange	Occurs when the user modifies the value of a form element

Window/document events:

Event	Description
onload	Occurs when the browser finishes the loading of all page elements
onunload	Occurs when the browser unloads current web page.
onresize	Occurs when the user resizes the browser window.

Adding/removing event to/from an element:

For adding and removing an event to/from an element, you can use **addEventListener(*event,***

***function, useCapture*)** and **removeEventListener(event, function)** methods.

Use 'click' instead of '**on**click' when you want to implement onclick event. Same for others as well;

Don't use any prefix **'on'** for event name.

Example:

<u>Main.html</u>

```html
<!doctype html>
<html lang="en">

<head>
    <meta charset="utf-8">
    <title>test program</title>
    <script src="./main.js" type="text/JavaScript"></script>
</head>

<body>

    <h2>JavaScript add/remove Event</h2>

    <button id="btn1">Add event on btn-2</button><br /><br />
    <button id="btn2">Button-2 (Please don't click me, I have no event
now)</button>
</body>

</html>
```

Main.js

```javascript
document.addEventListener("DOMContentLoaded", () => {
    let btn1 = document.getElementById("btn1");
    btn1.addEventListener("click", myFunction);
    let btn2 = document.getElementById("btn2");
    function myFunction() {
        if (btn1.textContent === "Add event on btn-2") {
            btn2.textContent = "Button-2 (Please click me, I have an event
now)";
            btn2.addEventListener("click", myFunction2);
            btn1.textContent = "Remove event from btn-2";
        }
        else {
            btn2.textContent = "Button-2 (Please don't click me, I have no
event now)";
            btn2.removeEventListener("click", myFunction2);
            btn1.textContent = "Add event on btn-2";
        }
    }
    function myFunction2() {
        alert("Hello!!!");
    }
});
```

Note:

1. The **useCapture** parameter of **addEventListener(*event, function, useCapture*)** method is optional to pass.

2. The ***useCapture*** parameter of **addEventListener(*event, function, useCapture*)** method is used for **event bubbling** and **event capturing**.

3. The default value of ***useCapture*** *is false means* event bubbling is the default behavious of JavaScript event.

Event Bubbling:

Event bubbling is a JavaScript concept, where an element receives an event and then bubbles up or propagates this event to its parent element or an ancestor element till the root element.

Event Capturing:

Event capturing is a JavaScript concept, where an element receives an event and then passed this event to its child element or an inner element till the last element of its hierarchy.

Let's discuss more about event bubbling and event capturing;

In below example we have two div, one inside another. The id of both div (parent and child) are 'outer' and 'inner' respectively.

Below is the Example:

<u>main.html</u>

```html
<!doctype html>
<html lang="en">

<head>
    <meta charset="utf-8">
    <title>test program</title>
    <script src="./main.js" type="text/JavaScript"></script>
</head>

<body>
    <h2>Example event bubbling/capturing</h2>
    <div id="outer">
        Parent div
        <div id="inner">
            Child div
        </div>
    </div>

    <style>
        div {
            color: white;
            font-size: 16px;
            font-weight: 700;
            text-align: center;
        }

        #outer {
            background-color: red;
            height: 200px;
        }

        #inner {
            background-color: blue;
            height: 100px;
            margin: 50px;
        }
    </style>
</body>

</html>
```

Example event bubbling/capturing

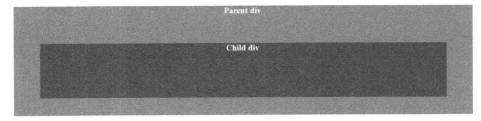

Now add click event on both divs by passing **useCapture** parameter as false (default value) or don't pass this parameter.

Main.js

```javascript
document.addEventListener("DOMContentLoaded", () => {
    //Parent div
    let outerDiv = document.getElementById("outer");
    outerDiv.addEventListener("click", () => {
        alert("Outer div");
    }, false);

    //Child div
    let innerDiv = document.getElementById("inner");
    innerDiv.addEventListener("click", () => {
        alert("Inner Div");
    }, false);
});
```

Now try to click on child (inner) div and observe the sequence of event raised.

You will see, inner Div's event occurs first before outer Div's event. Which means event bubbling is happening.

Let's try to pass **useCapture** parameter as true and see the differences:

main.js

```javascript
document.addEventListener("DOMContentLoaded", () => {
    //Parent div
    let outerDiv = document.getElementById("outer");
    outerDiv.addEventListener("click", () => {
        alert("Outer div");
    }, true);

    //Child div
    let innerDiv = document.getElementById("inner");
    innerDiv.addEventListener("click", () => {
        alert("Inner Div");
    }, true);
});
```

Let's refresh the browser and click on child (inner) div and observe the sequence of event raised.

You will see, outer Div's event occurs first before inner Div's event. Which means event capturing is happening.

Now the question is that, can we stop this default behavior or event bubbling and capturing?

Sure, we can stop this JavaScript behaviors, either using **stopPropagation()** or **stopImmediatePropagation()** methods as blow:

main.js

```javascript
document.addEventListener("DOMContentLoaded", () => {
    //Parent div
    let outerDiv = document.getElementById("outer");
    outerDiv.addEventListener("click", (event) => {
        event.stopPropagation();
        alert("Outer div");
    }, false);

    //Child div
    let innerDiv = document.getElementById("inner");
    innerDiv.addEventListener("click", (event) => {
        event.stopPropagation();
        alert("Inner Div");
    }, false);
});
```

Note:

1. stopPropagation will prevent **parent** handlers and **child** handlers from being executed.

2. stopImmediatePropagation will prevent parent handlers, **child** handler **and also** any **other** handlers on the same element from being executed.

Event Object:

A parameter specified in an event handler is called event object. You can see the same in previous example.

You can choose any name for this parameter. It automatically passes by the JavaScript when an event is occurred on an element.

It has some useful properties and methods based on the type of event handler; however, some are common for all.

Like: if you want to get the information about the element on which the event occurs.

You can use **target** property.

Let's see in action; in below example we will see how we can change the background color of an input box based on the entered valid color name else white/default background color will be display.

main.html

```html
<!doctype html>
<html lang="en">

<head>
    <meta charset="utf-8">
    <title>test program</title>
    <script src="./main.js" type="text/JavaScript"></script>
</head>

<body>
    <h2>Event Object Example</h2>
    <div id="outer">
        <input id="text_box" type="text" />
    </div>
</body>

</html>
```

main.js

```javascript
document.addEventListener("DOMContentLoaded", () => {
    //get input box and attached an event
    let text_box = document.getElementById("text_box");
    text_box.addEventListener("keyup", (event) => {
        event.stopPropagation();
        event.target.style.backgroundColor = event.target.value;
        console.log(event);
    }, false);

});
```

For more information you can log the event information in browser console as below:

console.log(event);

Event Object Example

Other ways to add an event on an element:

Using event handler properties:

you can also use event handler properties to assign the handler. But the issue is that you can't add more than one handler for a same event. Anything assigned later will overwrite earlier ones. Suppose, you want to call two different functions on an element click then you can implement the handler as below which will work fine:

element.addEventListener("click", function1);
element.addEventListener("click", function2);

But using property handler, you can only call one handler directly which is assigned later.

element.onclick = function1;
element.onclick = function2;

Here only function2 will be call when you click an element as **onclick** has the reference of function2 now.

Using inline event handler:

You can also use inline event handler on an element to implement the events.

However, this is not recommended way to use. Previous example can also be written as below;

main.html

```html
<!doctype html>
<html lang="en">

<head>
    <meta charset="utf-8">
    <title>test program</title>
    <script src="./main.js" type="text/JavaScript"></script>
</head>

<body>
    <h2>Event Object Example</h2>
    <div id="outer">
        <input id="text_box" type="text" onkeyup="updateColor(event)" />
    </div>
</body>

</html>
```

main.js

```javascript
function updateColor(event) {
    event.stopPropagation();
    event.target.style.backgroundColor = event.target.value;
    console.log(event);
};
```

In above example, you can see every time you press any character/key from key board, updateColor() method executes.

Which is absolutely not a good way to implement this requirement. Can you change this requirement based on some specific action or condition?

Like: Can you update the background color of input box only when a user would take a 1 sec break between the typing?

Sure, you can achieve this with the help of **JavaScript debouncing.**

Let's discuss two main concepts of JavaScript which is very useful to minimize the impact of user's frequently performed task. They will either impact the performance of application or not required in actual.

1. JavaScript debouncing
2. JavaScript throttling

1. JavaScript debouncing:

JavaScript debouncing is a concept to invoke a function after a defined period of time. The function will be invoked only if there is no other event is triggered with in that time. If the user triggers new event with in specified period of time, the timer will be reset.

JavaScript uses **setTimeout()** *and* **clearTimeout()** *methods to implement debouncing.*

Let's change the above example implement to updated color only if user would take 1sec time between the typing.

main.html

```
<!doctype html>
<html lang="en">

<head>
    <meta charset="utf-8">
    <title>test program</title>
    <script src="./main.js" type="text/JavaScript"></script>
</head>

<body>
    <h2>JavaScript Debouncing Example</h2>
    <div id="outer">
        <input id="text_box" type="text" />
    </div>
</body>

</html>
```

main.js

```javascript
document.addEventListener("DOMContentLoaded", () => {
    //timer variable
    let timer = null;
    //get input box and attached an event
    let text_box = document.getElementById("text_box");
    text_box.addEventListener("keyup", (event) => {
        event.stopPropagation();
        if (timer) {
            clearTimeout(timer); //reset the timer if user triggers new event
        }
        timer = setTimeout(() => { setColor(event) }, 1000); //setColor will
execute after 1 sec

    }, false);

    function setColor(event) {
        event.target.style.backgroundColor = event.target.value;
        console.log(event);
    }
});
```

In above example you can see the setColor function will only call when the user takes 1sec break after typing a character. See the log in browser console and observe the it only prints when a user pressed a key and wait for 1 sec to press the next key.

2. JavaScript throttling

The throttling is another useful concept of JavaScript. The 'throttling' invokes a function when an event triggers very first time and then wait for specified period of time to invoke the function again it skips all the new event triggers by the user with in that time.

JavaScript uses **setInterval()** and **clearInterval()** methods to implement throttling.

Let's see an example.

Suppose you want to submit your form data on a button (submit) click and uses an API to save the data at backend. This process takes some time for saving the data and returning the response. Meanwhile user can try to click 'submit' button again and again which may produce unwanted overhead for the application or multiple call for the API.

In such cases, it is better to use JavaScript throttling to implement the requirement.

In below example, you will see, the **saveData**() method only invoke very first time when you click 'submit' button and wouldn't invoke again for sub sequent event click with in 1 sec. It will only invoke again for very first click only after the specified time (1 sec) has passed or expired.

main.html

```html
<!doctype html>
<html lang="en">

<head>
    <meta charset="utf-8">
    <title>test program</title>
    <script src="./main.js" type="text/JavaScript"></script>
</head>

<body>
    <h2>JavaScript Debouncing Example</h2>
    <div id="outer">
        Enter Name :
        <input id="text_box" type="text" />
        <button id="submit">submit</button>
    </div>
</body>

</html>
```

Main.js

```javascript
document.addEventListener("DOMContentLoaded", () => {
    //timer variable
    let timer = null;
    //get input box
    let input_box = document.getElementById("text_box");
    //get button and attached an event
    let btnSubmit = document.getElementById("submit");
    btnSubmit.addEventListener("click", (event) => {
        event.stopPropagation();
        if (!timer) {
            saveData(input_box.value);
            timer = setInterval(() => {
                clearInterval(timer)
                timer = null;
            }, 1000); //saveData will only execute again after 1 sec
        }
        else {
            return;
        }

    }, false);

    function saveData(name) {
        console.log(name)
    }
});
```

In above example, enter name and then click submit again and again, see the log in browser console and observe that the name in console only prints when a user clicks first time and wait for 1 sec to invoke the same function again and print the name again.

You can also increase the delay time value to observe the delay.

Browser Storage Mechanism:

Below are some important mechanisms to store a small piece of data on browser.

1. cookie
2. localStorage
3. sessionStorage

1. Cookie

A cookie is a small piece of information stored at client system by the browser at the time of browsing a page.

This is very useful in case of website to store user preferences like theme color, input   and more.

A user can change their browser setting to accept, reject or delete cookies. A cookie can   store data up to 4 KB.

You can set and get a cookie in JavaScript using **document.cookie** property.

Example:

main.html:

```html
<!doctype html>
<html lang="en">

<head>
    <meta charset="utf-8">
    <title>test program</title>
    <script src="./main.js" type="text/JavaScript"></script>
</head>

<body>
    <h2>Cookie Example</h2>
    <div id="outer">
        User Name :
        <input type="text" id="userName" /> <br /><br />
        Password :
        <input type="password" id="password" /><br /><br />
        <button id="setCookie">Set cookie</button>
        <button id="getCookie">Get Cookie</button><br /><br />
        <div id="result"></div>
    </div>
</body>

</html>
```

main.js

```javascript
document.addEventListener("DOMContentLoaded", () => {

    //get DOM elements
    let setCookieBtn = document.getElementById("setCookie");
    let getCookieBtn = document.getElementById("getCookie");
    let userName = document.getElementById("userName");
    let password = document.getElementById("password");
    let result = document.getElementById("result");

    //add events
    setCookieBtn.addEventListener("click", () => {
        //set cookie
        document.cookie = `UserName=${userName.value}`;
        document.cookie = `Password=${password.value}`;
    })

    getCookieBtn.addEventListener("click", () => {
        //get cookie
        let cookies = document.cookie.split(";");

        let _name = `UserName = ${cookies[0].replace("UserName=", '')}`;
        let _password = `Password = ${cookies[1].replace("Password=", '')}`;
        result.innerHTML = `Below are the cookies value
<br/>${_name}<br/>${_password}`
    })
});
```

Run the above example and clic setCookie button first and then getCookie.

You will observe the result as below.

Please try above example with **Mozilla** browser, others browser may not create cookie for local

pages.

2. **localStorage**

localStorage is used to store the data for each given origin that persists even a browser is closed or reopen.

Stored data never expires, you can clear this using JavaScript or clearing the browser local stored data.

localStorage can store the data up to 5 MB.

You can get the number of data items stored in the localStorage using length property of localStorage (**localStorage.length**).

Below are the useful methods of localStorage :

clear(): It clears all key/value out of the storage.

Example:

```
localStorage.clear();
```

getItem(): It returns the value of the specified key

Example:

```
localStorage.getItem("key")
```

key(): It returns the name of the nth key

Example:

```
localStorage.key(2);
```

setItem(): It Adds/modifies a key to the storage with the given value.

Example:

```
localStorage.setItem("key","value")
```

removeItem(): It removes specified key from the storage.

Example:

```
localStorage.removeItem("key")
```

Please try to run below example for more understanding:

main.html

```html
<!doctype html>
<html lang="en">

<head>
    <meta charset="utf-8">
    <title>test program</title>
    <script src="./main.js" type="text/JavaScript"></script>
</head>

<body>
    <h2>localStorage Example</h2>
    <div id="outer">
        User Name :
        <input type="text" id="userName" /> <br /><br />
        Password :
        <input type="password" id="password" /><br /><br />
        <button id="setItem">Set item</button>
        <button id="getItem">Get item</button><br /><br />
        <button id="removeItem">Remove item (UsenName)</button>
        <button id="clearAllItem">Clear all items</button><br /><br />
        <div id="resull"></div>
    </div>
</body>

</html>
```

main.js

```javascript
document.addEventListener("DOMContentLoaded", () => {

    //get DOM elements
    let setItem = document.getElementById("setItem");
    let getItem = document.getElementById("getItem");
    let removeItem = document.getElementById("removeItem");
    let clearAllItem = document.getElementById("clearAllItem");
    let userName = document.getElementById("userName");
    let password = document.getElementById("password");
    let result = document.getElementById("result");

    //add events
    setItem.addEventListener("click", () => {
        //set items
        localStorage.setItem("UserName", userName.value);
        localStorage.setItem("Password", password.value);
    })
```

```
getItem.addEventListener("click", () => {
        //get items
        if (localStorage.length > 0) {
            let _name = `UserName = ${localStorage.getItem("UserName")}`;
            let _password = `Password = ${localStorage.getItem("Password")}`;
            result.innerHTML = `Below are the cookies value
<br/>${_name}<br/>${_password}`
        }
        else {
            result.innerHTML = "No item found in localStorage.";
        }
    })

    removeItem.addEventListener("click", () => {
        //get items
        if (localStorage.length > 0 && localStorage.getItem("UserName")) {
            localStorage.removeItem("UserName")
            result.innerHTML = `Item deleted with key = UserName.`
        }
        else {
            result.innerHTML = "No item found in localStorage with key =
UserName.";
        }
    })

    clearAllItem.addEventListener("click", () => {
        //clear all items
        localStorage.clear();
        result.innerHTML = "All item deleted from localStorage.";
    })
});
```

Run the above example and observe the result.

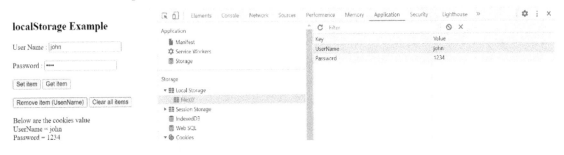

3. sessionStorage

sessionStorage is same as localStorage but the data persists only for a session meaning data automatically removes when a browser (or tab) is closed.

It has same properties and methods as localStorage.

Try to run the above example just replacing the **localStorage** with **sessionStorage** and see the result in browser.

Revise JavaScript important features using programs:

In this section we will revise some important JavaScript features with the help of programs. We will not say that we will see all approaches to implement a program or requirement. Our main focus is, revise JavaScript features/concepts with the help of these programs.

Below is the list of programs:

1. Write a function with a parameter, which will return true if parameter is convertible to a number else return false.

To implement the above requirement or function you can use isNaN() global function of JavaScript which returns true if a parameter is convertible to number else returns false.

Implementation:

```
function isNumber(num) {
    return !isNaN(num);
}
console.log(isNumber(20)); //true
console.log(isNumber("20")); //true
console.log(isNumber("-20")); //true
console.log(isNumber("20y")); //false
```

2. Write a function with a percentage parameter which will return first if percentage >= 60, second if percentage >= 45, pass if percentage >= 35 else return fail.

To implement the above requirement or function you can use if...else if...else conditional statement of ternary operator.

Implementation (using if...else if...else)

```
function getResult(percentage) {
    if (percentage >= 60) {
        return 'First';
    }
    else if (percentage >= 45) {
        return 'Second';
    }
    else if (percentage >= 35) {
        return 'Pass';
    }
    else {
        return 'Fail';
    }
}

console.log(getResult(70)); //First
console.log(getResult(55)); //Second
console.log(getResult(40)); //Pass
console.log(getResult(30)); //Fail
```

Implementation (using ternary operator)

```
function getResult(percentage) {
    return (percentage >= 60 ? 'First' :
        percentage >= 45 ? 'Second' :
            percentage >= 35 ? 'Pass' : 'Fail');
}


console.log(getResult(70)); //First
console.log(getResult(55)); //Second
console.log(getResult(40)); //Pass
console.log(getResult(30)); //Fail
```

3. Write a function with three parametes (string, subString, replaceWith) which will replace all the occurrences of subString with replaceWith and then return modified string.

To implement the above requirement or function, you can use String's replace method where you can pass first parameter as a regex.

Implementation:

```
function replaceStr(str, subStr, replaceWith) {
    let reg = new RegExp(subStr, "g");
    let newStr = str.replace(reg, replaceWith);
    return newStr;
}

console.log(replaceStr("Hello! how do you do?", "do", "Doo")); //Hello! how
Doo you Doo?
console.log(replaceStr("good morning?", "o", "i")); //giid mirning?
```

In above example we used regex to pass first parameter in replace method because passing a simple string only replace first occurrence of sub string.

4. Write a function which will allow user to add n numbers.

To implement the above requirement or function, you can use one of below ways:

Using arguments array:

```
function add() {
    let sum = 0;
    for (let num of arguments) {
        sum += num;
    }
    return sum;
}


console.log(add(1, 2, 3)); //6
console.log(add(1, 2, 3, 4, 5, 6)); //21
```

Using rest parameter:

```
function add(...numbers) {
    let sum = 0;
    for (let num of numbers) {
        sum += num;
    }
    return sum;
}


console.log(add(1, 2, 3)); //6
console.log(add(1, 2, 3, 4, 5, 6)); //21
```

Using function currying:

```
function add(num1) {
    return function (num2) {
        if (!num2) {
            return num1;
        }
        else {
            return add(num1 + num2)
        }
    }
}

console.log(add(1)(2)(3)()); //6
console.log(add(1)(2)(3)(4)(5)(6)()); //21
```

5. Write a function for swapping 2 numbers.

To implement above requirement, you one of the below ways:

Using addition and difference:

```
function swapNumber(num1, num2) {
    console.log(`Before swap: ${num1}, ${num2}`) //Before swap: 10, 20
    num1 = num1 + num2;
    num2 = num1 - num2;
    num1 = num1 - num2;
    console.log(`After swap: ${num1}, ${num2}`) //After swap: 20, 10
}

swapNumber(10, 20);
```

Using array destructuring:

```javascript
function swapNumber(num1, num2) {
    console.log(`Before swap: ${num1}, ${num2}`); //Before swap: 10, 20
    [num1, num2] = [num2, num1];
    console.log(`After swap: ${num1}, ${num2}`); //After swap: 20, 10
}

swapNumber(10, 20);
```

Using XOR:

```javascript
function swapNumber(num1, num2) {
    console.log(`Before swap: ${num1}, ${num2}`); //Before swap: 10, 20
    num1 = num1 ^ num2;
    num2 = num1 ^ num2;
    num1 = num1 ^ num2;
    console.log(`After swap: ${num1}, ${num2}`); //After swap: 20, 10
}

swapNumber(10, 20);
```

6. Write a function to convert base 10 number to base 8.

To implement the above function or requirement, you can use toString() method with the base parameter to convert a number with the specified base.

```javascript
function convertToBase(number, base) {
    return number.toString(base);
}

console.log(convertToBase(20, 8)); //24
console.log(convertToBase(30, 8)); //36
```

7. Write a function with 2 parameters (string, subString) which will return index of subString if subString is present in string else return –1.

To implement the above requirement, you can use indexOf() method of string.

```
function getIndexOfSubString(str, subString) {
    return str.indexOf(subString);
}

console.log(getIndexOfSubString("Hi! how are you?", "are")); //8
console.log(getIndexOfSubString("Hi! how are you?", "hello")); //-1
```

8. Write a function to remove duplicate values from an array.

To implement the above requirement/function, you can use one of below ways:

Creating new array with loop:

```
function removeDuplicate(arr) {
    let uniqueArr = [];
    for (let item of arr) {
        if (uniqueArr.indexOf(item) < 0) {
            uniqueArr.push(item);
        }
    }
    return uniqueArr;
}

console.log(removeDuplicate([2, 3, 4, 5, 2, 3, 7])); //[ 2, 3, 4, 5, 7 ]
console.log(removeDuplicate(["Hi", "Hello", "GM", "Hi", "GM"])); //[ 'Hi',
'Hello', 'GM' ]
```

Using filter method of array:

```
function removeDuplicate(arr) {
    return arr.filter((ele, index, arr) => arr.indexOf(ele) === index);
}

console.log(removeDuplicate([2, 3, 4, 5, 2, 3, 7])); //[ 2, 3, 4, 5, 7 ]
console.log(removeDuplicate(["Hi", "Hello", "GM", "Hi", "GM"])); //[ 'Hi',
'Hello', 'GM' ]
```

Using Set object with destructuring:

```
function removeDuplicate(arr) {
    let [...unique] = new Set(arr).values();
    return unique;
}

console.log(removeDuplicate([2, 3, 4, 5, 2, 3, 7])); //[ 2, 3, 4, 5, 7 ]
console.log(removeDuplicate(["Hi", "Hello", "GM", "Hi", "GM"])); //[ 'Hi',
'Hello', 'GM' ]
```

9. Write a function to concatenate 2 or more arrays.

To implement the above requirement or function, you can either use array concat() method or JavaScript spread(...) operator.

Using concat method:

```
function joinArray(arr1, arr2, arr3) {
    return arr1.concat(arr2, arr3);
}

console.log(joinArray([2, 3], [4, 5], [6, 7])); //[ 2, 3, 4, 5, 7 ]
console.log(joinArray(["Hi", "Hello"], ["GM", "Hi"], ["GM"])); //[ 'Hi',
'Hello', 'GM' ]
```

Using spead(...) operator:

```
function joinArray(arr1, arr2, arr3) {
    return [...arr1, ...arr2, ...arr3];
}
console.log(joinArray([2, 3], [4, 5], [6, 7])); //[ 2, 3, 4, 5, 7 ]
console.log(joinArray(["Hi", "Hello"], ["GM", "Hi"], ["GM"])); //[ 'Hi',
'Hello', 'GM' ]
```

10. Write a function with an array parameter, which will return a new array after multiply each element by 2.

To implement above requirement, you can you one of below ways:

Implement with simple loop:

```
function multiplyBy2(arr) {
    let newArr = [];
    for (let item of arr) {
        newArr.push(item * 2);
    }
    return newArr;
}

console.log(multiplyBy2([2, 3])); //[ 4, 6 ]
console.log(multiplyBy2([5, 6])); //[ 10, 12 ]
```

Implement with map() function:

```
function multiplyBy2(arr) {
    return arr.map(ele => ele * 2)
}

console.log(multiplyBy2([2, 3])); //[ 4, 6 ]
console.log(multiplyBy2([5, 6])); //[ 10, 12 ]
```

11. Write a function with an array parameter, which will return a new array with all items is greater than 10.

To implement the above requirement or function, you can use one of below ways:

Using simple loop and conditional statements:

```
function GetAllNumberGreaterThan10(arr) {
    let newArr = [];
    for (let item of arr) {
        if (item > 10) {
            newArr.push(item);
        }
    }
    return newArr;
}

console.log(GetAllNumberGreaterThan10([15, 5, 7, 20])); //[ 15, 20 ]
console.log(GetAllNumberGreaterThan10([10, 20, 30])); //[ 20, 30 ]
```

Using filter() method of array:

```
function GetAllNumberGreaterThan10(arr) {
    return arr.filter(ele => ele > 10);
}

console.log(GetAllNumberGreaterThan10([15, 5, 7, 20])); //[ 15, 20 ]
console.log(GetAllNumberGreaterThan10([10, 20, 30])); //[ 20, 30 ]
```

12. Write a function with an array parameter, which will return sum of all array's items.

To implement the above requirement, you can use one of below ways:

Using simple loop:

```
function sumOfArr(arr) {
    let sum = 0;
    for (let item of arr) {
        sum += item;
    }
    return sum;
}

console.log(sumOfArr([15, 5, 7, 20])); //47
console.log(sumOfArr([10, 20, 30])); //60
```

Using array reduce() method:

```
function sumOfArr(arr) {
    return arr.reduce((acc, ele) => acc + ele);
}

console.log(sumOfArr([15, 5, 7, 20])); //47
console.log(sumOfArr([10, 20, 30])); //60
```

13. Write a function with a complex object parameter, which will print all the properties and their respective values.

To implement the above requirement, you can use one of the below ways:

Using getOwnPropertyNames() or Keys method:

```javascript
function PrintPropertiesAndValues(obj) {
    let properties = Object.getOwnPropertyNames(obj); //you can also use
Object.keys(obj)
    for (let prop of properties) {
        let value = obj[prop];
        if (value instanceof Object) {
            PrintPropertiesAndValues(value);
        }
        else {
            console.log(`${prop} = ${obj[prop]}`)
        }
    }
}

const address = {
    city: "Noida",
    country: "India"
}
const person = {
    firstName: "John",
    lastName: "Petro",
    address: { ...address }
}
PrintPropertiesAndValues(address);
console.log("_____")
PrintPropertiesAndValues(person);
  //output:
  //city = Noida
  //country = India
  //_____
  //firstName = John
  //lastName = Petro
  //city = Noida
  //country = India
```

Using for...in loop:

```
function PrintPropertiesAndValues(obj) {
    for (let prop in obj) {
        let value = obj[prop];
        if (value instanceof Object) {
            PrintPropertiesAndValues(value);
        }
        else {
            console.log(`${prop} = ${obj[prop]}`)
        }
    }
}

const address = {
    city: "Noida",
    country: "India"
}
const person = {
    firstName: "John",
    lastName: "Petro",
    address: { ...address }
}
PrintPropertiesAndValues(address);
console.log("_____")
PrintPropertiesAndValues(person);
  //output:
  //city = Noida
  //country = India
  //_____
  //firstName = John
  //lastName = Petro
  //city = Noida
  //country = India
```

14. Write a function with an array parameter (array of object [id, name]), which will return a sorted array based on id value.

To implement above requirement or function, you can use sort method() of array:

```
function sortByName(persons) {
    return persons.sort((p1, p2) => p1.name >= p2.name ? 0 : -1)
}


let persons = [];
let names = ["John", "Petro", "Peter", "Pepo", "Jonson"]
for (let i = 1; i <= 10; i++) {
    persons.push({
        id: i,
        name: `${names[i % 5]}`
    })
}
console.log("Before sort-");
console.log(persons);
console.log("After sort-");
console.log(sortByName(persons));
 //output;
 //Before sort-
 //[
 //   { id: 1, name: 'Petro' },
 //   { id: 2, name: 'Peter' },
 //   { id: 3, name: 'Pepo' },
 //   { id: 4, name: 'Jonson' },
 //   { id: 5, name: 'John' },
 //   { id: 6, name: 'Petro' },
 //   { id: 7, name: 'Peter' },
 //   { id: 8, name: 'Pepo' },
 //   { id: 9, name: 'Jonson' },
 //   { id: 10, name: 'John' }
 //]
 //After sort-
 //[
 //   { id: 5, name: 'John' },
 //   { id: 10, name: 'John' },
 //   { id: 4, name: 'Jonson' },
 //   { id: 9, name: 'Jonson' },
 //   { id: 3, name: 'Pepo' },
 //   { id: 8, name: 'Pepo' },
 //   { id: 2, name: 'Peter' },
 //   { id: 7, name: 'Peter' },
 //   { id: 1, name: 'Petro' },
 //   { id: 6, name: 'Petro' }
 //]
```

15. Write a custom function, which will work same as map function of array.

To implement the custom map function which will work same as map() function of array.

You need to create a array prototype method with the same parameters and functionality as map().

Please understand the map() method of array first before checking the below implementation.

```
//declare a prototype function with a callback function parameter
Array.prototype.myMap = function (callback) {
    let arr = [];
    this.forEach((item, index) => {
        arr.push(callback(item, index, this))
    })
    return arr;
}


let arr = [2, 3, 4];
let newArr = arr.myMap(function (item, index, arr) {
    return item * item * item;
});
console.log(newArr); // [ 8, 27, 64 ]
```

16. Write a custom function, which will work same as filter function of array.

To implement the custom filter function which will work same as filter() function of array.

You need to create a array prototype method with the same parameters and functionality as filter().

Please understand the filter() method of array first before checking the below implementation.

```
//declare a prototype function with a callback function parameter
Array.prototype.myFilter = function (callback) {
    let arr = [];
    this.forEach((item, index) => {
        if (callback(item, index, this)) {
            arr.push(item);
        }
    })
    return arr;
}

let arr = [10, 20, 15, 25, 5];
let newArr = arr.myFilter(function (item, index, arr) {
    return item > 10;
});
console.log(newArr); //[ 20, 15, 25 ]
```

17. Write a custom function, which will work same as reduce function of array.

To implement the custom filter function which will work same as reduce() function of array.

You need to create a array prototype method with the same parameters and functionality as reduce().

Please understand the reduce() method of array first before checking the below implementation.

```javascript
//declare a prototype function with a callback function and initial value
parameters
Array.prototype.myReduce = function (callback, initialValue) {
    let result = initialValue ? initialValue : this[0];
    this.forEach((item, index) => {
        if (index > 0 || initialValue) {
            result = callback(result, item, index, this);
        }
    })
    return result;
}

let arr = [1, 2, 3];
let result = arr.myReduce(function (acc, item, index, arr) {
    return acc - item;
}); //without initial value
console.log(result); //-4
result = arr.myReduce(function (acc, item, index, arr) {
    return acc - item;
}, 10); //with initial value
console.log(result); //4
```

18. Write a function, which will execute after every 2 seconds.

To implement the above requirement or function, you can use setInterval() method.

```javascript
function sayHello() {
    console.log("Hello! JavaScript.");
    //any other code
}

setInterval(sayHello, 2000);
```

Above example will print 'Hello! JavaScript' in every 2 seconds.

19. Write a function, which will execute once after 2 seconds.

To implement the above requirement or function, you can use setTimeout() method of JavaScript.

```
function sayHello() {
    console.log("Hello! JavaScript.");
    //any other code
}

setTimeout(sayHello, 2000);
```

Above example will print 'Hello! JavaScript' after 2 seconds.

20. Write a function with a string URL parameter, which will call a get API before returning the result.

To implement above requirement, use fetch() API to get data as below:

```
function getActivity(api_url) {
    let options = {
        method: 'GET'
    }
    try {
        let result = await fetch(api_url, options);
        let data = await result.json();
        console.log(data);
    }
    catch {
        console.log("An error occured in API.")
    }
}

getActivity("GET_API_URL");
```

In above example, you can pass any get api url in getActivity() method. It will return the result and will log in console.

21. Write a function, which will print all the even numbers between 1-50.

To implement the above requirement or function, you can use one of below ways:

Using loop:

```
function getEven(lastNum) {
    let evenArr = [];
    for (let i = 1; i <= lastNum; i++) {
        if (i % 2 === 0) {
            evenArr.push(i);
        }
    }
    return evenArr;
}

console.log(getEven(50)); //[ 2,  4,  6,  8, 10, 12, 14, 16, 18, 20, 22, 24,
26, 28, 30, 32, 34, 36, 38, 40, 42, 44, 46, 48, 50 ]
```

Using keys() and map() methods of array:

```
function getEven(lastNum) {
    return [...Array(lastNum + 1).keys()].filter(ele => ele > 0 && ele % 2 ===
0);
}
console.log(getEven(50)); //[ 2,  4,  6,  8, 10, 12, 14, 16, 18, 20, 22, 24,
26, 28, 30, 32, 34, 36, 38, 40, 42, 44, 46, 48, 50 ]
```

22. Create a web page to change a div color based on the selected color in drop down.

To implement the above requirement, you can use <select></select> HTML element and implement the onchange event to set the div color.Please check the below implementation:

Main.html

```html
<!doctype html>
<html lang="en">

<head>
    <meta charset="utf-8">
    <title>test program</title>
    <script src="./main.js" type="text/JavaScript"></script>
</head>

<body>
    <h2>Change color Example</h2>
    <div id="mainDiv">
        <select id="select_color">
            <option disabled selected>Select color</option>
            <option>Green</option>
            <option>Red</option>
            <option>Blue</option>
        </select>
    </div>
    <style>
        #select_color {
            width: 200px;
            font-size: 18px;
        }
    </style>
</body>

</html>
```

```
document.addEventListener("DOMContentLoaded", () => {

    //get DOM elements
    let selectColor = document.getElementById("select_color");
    let body = document.querySelector("body");

    //add events
    selectColor.addEventListener("change", () => {
        //set color
        body.style.backgroundColor = selectColor.value;
    })
});
```

Now, open the HTML page in any browser and observe the result as:

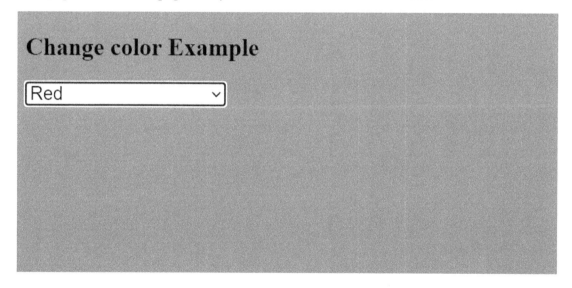

23. Create a web page with an input box, which will not allow 'K' key to enter.

To implement above requirement, you can use onkeydown event as below:

main.html

```html
<!doctype html>
<html lang="en">

<head>
    <meta charset="utf-8">
    <title>test program</title>
    <script src="./main.js" type="text/JavaScript"></script>
</head>

<body>
    <h2>Prevent a key to enter example</h2>
    <div id="mainDiv">
        This input box will not accept key 'k'.
        <input type="text" id="input_box" />
    </div>
</body>

</html>
```

main.js

```javascript
document.addEventListener("DOMContentLoaded", () => {

    //get DOM elements
    let input_box = document.getElementById("input_box");

    //add events
    input_box.addEventListener("keydown", (event) => {
        console.log(event)
        if (event.key === 'k' || event.key === 'K') {
            event.preventDefault();
        }
    })
});
```

Open the above example in any browser and observe the behavior.

Prevent a key to enter example

this input box will not accept key 'k'. [   ]

24. Create a web page with a button (add input box) to add one input box and a delete button each time when a user clicks on it.

Please check the below example for better understanding.

main.html

```html
<!doctype html>
<html lang="en">

<head>
    <meta charset="utf-8">
    <title>test program</title>
    <script src="./main.js" type="text/JavaScript"></script>
</head>

<body>
    <h2>Add Dynamic Element Example</h2>
    <div id="mainDiv">
        Click below button to add an input box.
        <input type="button" id="btn" value="Add (+) input box" /><br /><br />
    </div>
</body>

</html>
```

main.js

```javascript
document.addEventListener("DOMContentLoaded", () => {

    //get DOM elements
    let btn = document.getElementById("btn");
    let mainDiv = document.getElementById("mainDiv");

    //add events
    let i = 1;
    btn.addEventListener("click", (event) => {
        //create an input box to body
        let input = document.createElement("input");
        input.setAttribute('type', 'text');
        input.setAttribute('value', 'text' + i);
        let btnDelete = document.createElement("input");
        btnDelete.setAttribute('type', 'button');
        btnDelete.setAttribute("value", "Delete (-)");
        btnDelete.addEventListener("click", () => {
            mainDiv.removeChild(btnDelete.nextSibling);
            mainDiv.removeChild(btnDelete);
            mainDiv.removeChild(input);
        })
        let br = document.createElement("br");
        mainDiv.append(input, btnDelete, br);
        i++;
    })
});
```

Open the above created page in any browser and observe the behavior.

Add Dynamic Element Example

Click button to add an input box. | Add (+) input box |

text1	Delete (-)
text2	Delete (-)
text3	Delete (-)

25. Create a web page to display mouse position (x, y) as tooltip.

Please check the below implementation for achieving above requirement.

main.html

```html
<!doctype html>
<html lang="en">

<head>
    <meta charset="utf-8">
    <title>test program</title>
    <script src="./main.js" type="text/JavaScript"></script>
</head>

<body>
    <h2>Mouse location example</h2>
    <div id="mainDiv">
        <div id="divTooltip">

        </div>
    </div>
    <style>
        #mainDiv {
            min-height: 200px;
            border: solid 2px black;
            background-color: gray;
        }

        #divTooltip {
            padding: 5px;
            border: solid 2px red;
            border-radius: 5px;
            background-color: pink;
            position: absolute;
            display: none;
        }
    </style>
</body>

</html>
```

main.js

```javascript
document.addEventListener("DOMContentLoaded", () => {

    //get DOM elements
    let mainDiv = document.getElementById("mainDiv");
    let tooltip = document.getElementById("divTooltip");

    //add events
    mainDiv.addEventListener("mousemove", (event) => {
        tooltip.style.display = "block";
        tooltip.style.top = event.y + "px";
        tooltip.style.left = event.x + "px";
        tooltip.innerHTML = `x = ${event.x}<br/>y = ${event.y}`
    });

    mainDiv.addEventListener("mouseout", () => {
        tooltip.style.display = 'none';
    })
});
```

Open the above created page in any browser and observe the behavior.

Mouse location example

Thank You!!!